Living Life With Conscious Intention

Living Life With Conscious Intention

Key behaviors for enriching your
life and the world we live in

by

W. Marie Giles

Living Life With Conscious Intention

Published by Willie M. Giles

Copyright 2012 by W. Marie Giles

All rights reserved. No part of this book may be used or reproduced in any manner whatsoever without the written permission of the Publisher.

Unless otherwise noted, scripture taken from the HOLY BIBLE, NEW INTERNATIONAL VERSION. Copyright 1973, 1978, 1984 by International Bible Society. Used by permission of Zondervan Publishing House. All rights reserved.

The "NIV" and "New International Version" trademarks are registered in the United States Patent and Trademark Office by International Bible Society. Use of either trademark requires the permission of International Bible Society.

Library of Congress Control Number: 2012941398

ISBN: 978-0-9728944-2-5
Cover design: W. Marie Giles
Book layout design: W. Marie Giles

Printed in the United States of America

Other Books By W. Marie Giles

Open Your Mind, Open Your Heart: A collection of words of wisdom, heartfelt thoughts, and original poetry

Pay Attention To Your Life: Reflections on self-awareness and self-determination

Comments on W. Marie Giles books

"Everyday I experience tough decisions, emotional battles and spiritual quests and this book along with the Bible has helped me stay focus[ed] on spirit and man, on right and wrong, and on good and bad. I thank the writer for making my way easier through the sharing of such powerful insights and compassion." — P. N.

"This book expresses, in simple words, rich lessons that create a happier and more responsible life. The author, with warm and sincere openness, does a remarkable job of implicitly encouraging the reader to examine his own personal relationships with self, family, friends, community...world - to create a more positive outcome." — D. S.

"This wonderful book touches the inner soul. You identify with each passage as you dissolve into reading." — H. B.

"It is written that you should hide the Word of God in your heart so that you will speak and live that which is in your heart. As you read this book, "Open Your Mind, Open Your Heart", you will enjoy the fullness of living spiritually strong and to live spiritually strong your mind has to stay positive to endure all of life's problems and concerns." — M. A.

"In reading this book, I traveled on a wonderful and thought inspiring journey of a reaffirmation of life. Marie Giles opened her heart and soul to eloquently pour on to the written page what most of us would find a struggle just to bring forth in a coherent thought. " —T. C.

"Purposefulness is having conscious" intention. It is having a clear focus on what you are doing and why you are doing it ."
— Unknown

Acknowledgement

As always, I am grateful for God's insights on the true purpose of my life.

I wish to thank my family and friends for their confidence and interest in my writing projects over the past years, as well as their encouragement and support.

I am also grateful to my former co-workers for their support and continued interest.

Without such individuals in our lives, to cheer us on, when we make a decision to endeavor in areas where many don't feel they can succeed, who knows where any of us would be.

Thank you all for making this possible.

Foreword

We all should constantly strive to maintain awareness of our thoughts, actions, and words, and the impact—either negative or positive—they have on us and others with whom we interact. We are not perfect when it comes to this behavior, but if we continue to try and get better each day with every interaction, we will see progress.

I came up with the idea and title for this book while paying close attention to my own behavior, thoughts, and actions, as well as that of others. I wanted to write this book to share some of my own solutions and practices which allow me to stay in the moment for the majority of the time. In doing so, I make constant efforts to remain "awake" to the things that matter most in life.

I use the term "awake" to indicate my belief in the message of several books I have read over the past years. *The Four Agreements: A Practical Guide to Personal Freedom, A Toltec Wisdom Book*, by don Miguel Ruiz, tells us that we each live inside our own dream. As a result, we interact with others, and ourselves, based on this reality. We are encouraged to realize our own dream as well as that of others. We must be aware of when we get pulled into the dream or dreams of others, thereby abandoning our own. We are also encouraged to awaken from our own dreams and see what is real.

In his book, *A New Earth: Awakening To Your Life's Purpose,* Eckhart Tolle shares with us the need for a "shift in consciousness" which represents an awakening. According to Tolle, transcending our ego-based state of consciousness is not only essential to personal happiness but also the key to ending the conflict and suffering throughout the world."

Another author who speaks of "awakening" as a challenging, yet liberating pursuit, is Mark Nepo, author of *The Book of Awakening: Having the Life You Want By Being Present to the Life You Have.* He has gained a level of mindfulness, after battling cancer, that encouraged me to dig deeper into my own pursuit of conscious intention.

As a result of studying these and numerous other authors who inspire this message, I wanted to share my views and practices with those who would take the time to read my words. I hope I can encourage you to embark upon your own journey toward an awakening to enrich your life as well as making a positive and enduring difference in the world in which we live.

It is important to me that you understand, upfront, this is not a book of "how-to" steps that you follow and miraculously become consciously intent. This is a book which encourages you to look at your own consciousness, and how it guides your intentions, in order to become better and improve the world in which we all live.

Dedication

To the memory of my dear mother who passed on in July 2001. I am truly blessed to have had her in my life. She taught me many life lessons that she probably never knew she had.

For Helen (Jeanne) - my dear sister, who passed on in December 2007: You were always such an inspiration to me and you always will be.

For Henry, Hendric, and Westin—You are my reasons for being.

To all who would dare to endeavor into the unknown (and known) areas of their day-to-day lives, in search of a means of getting out of their dreams and living a life fully awake with an awareness of their words, actions, thoughts, and habits that impact themselves and others around the world.

About the Author

W. Marie Giles recently retired from the Federal Civil Service in the field of Information Technology where she advanced to senior management during her 30-year career.

Marie has been on a journey of self-discovery and self-improvement nearly all her life. She has come to realize the journey does not end, for "it is in the journey that you continue to improve your outlook and reach a higher level of fulfillment." She also realizes the journey pauses at many destinations throughout our many phases of life. Conscious Intention allows her to be ready for each and every event along the way.

Marie is also the author of *Open Your Mind, Open Your Heart: A collection of words of wisdom, heartfelt thoughts, and original poetry* and *Pay Attention To Your Life: Reflections on self-awareness and self-determination,* both available for purchase from amazon.com or direct from the author.

TABLE OF CONTENTS

Acknowledgement vi

Foreword vii

Dedication ix

About the author x

Part I — Living Life with Conscious Intention

Chapter 1—Introduction   1

Chapter 2—Conscious Intention is a Choice   5

Chapter 3—Conscious Intention Must be Practiced   9

Chapter 4—Conscious Intention Requires Awakening   13

Chapter 5—Conscious Intention Activities   17

Part II — Key Behaviors for enriching our lives

1. Be Accepting   26

2. Be Accommodating   28

3. Be Accountable   30

4. Show Appreciation   32

5. Give Attention   34

6. Maintain Balance   36

7. Believe in Something   38

8. Get Better   40

9. Observe Boundaries   42

10. Stay Calm   44

11. Provide Clear Expectations   46

12. Be Committed   48

13. Show Compassion   50

14. Engage In Continuous Learning   52

15. Be Devoted   54

16. Value Diversity   56

17. Follow Your Dreams   58

18. Show Emotional Control   60

19. Embrace Life   62

20. Encourage Others   64

21. Strive For Excellence   66

22. Execute Your Plans   68

23. Have Faith   70

24. Be Flexible   72

25. Follow Through   74

26. Follow Up   76

27. Practice Forgiveness   78

28. Practice Generosity   80

29. Be Gentle   82

30. Become Goal-oriented   84

31. Be Helpful   86

32. Be Honest   88

33. Have Hope   90

34. Practice Humility   92

35. Have A Sense Of Humor   94

36. Use Your Imagination   96

37. Show Initiative   98

38. Have Integrity   100

39. Be Just   102

40. Be Joyful   104

41. Practice Kindness   106

42. Listen   108

43. Love   110

44. Show Loyalty   112

45. Be Memorable   114

46. Be Ever Mindful   116

47. Be Non-judging   118

48. Be Objective   120

49. Be Open-hearted   122

50. Be Open-minded   124

51. Have Patience   126

52. Keep A Positive Attitude   128

53. Give Praise   130

54. Believe In Prayer   132

55. Find Your Purpose   134

56. Show Respect   136

57. Accept Responsibility   138

58. Practice Self-discipline   140

59. Develop Self-awareness   142

60. Practice Sharing   144

61. Show Tenderness   146

62. Think First   148

63. Learn To Trust   150

64. Be Trustworthy   152

65. Try Harder   154

66. Have Some Understanding   156

67. Value Life   158

68. Show Willingness   160

69. Gain Wisdom   162

70. Maintain A Sense Of Wonder   164

71. Work Harder   166

72. Stay Young At Heart   168

73. Learn To Yield   170

74. Maintain Zeal   172

Afterword   175

Additional Resources   176

Part I: Living Life With Conscious Intention

Conscious

The quality or state of being aware especially of something within oneself; the state or fact of being conscious of an external object, state, or fact

Intention

A determination to act in a certain way

Chapter 1
Introduction

"Intention is the core of all conscious life. It is our intentions that create karma, our intentions that help others, our intentions that lead us away from the delusions of individuality toward the immutable verities of enlightened awareness. Conscious intention colors and moves everything. -- Master Hsing Yun

What is Conscious Intention?

Conscious Intention is *the quality or state of being aware of our determination to behave or act in a certain manner with regard to ourselves and others.* It is knowing, within ourselves, what we are thinking about saying or doing, why we want to say or do it, and its impact on the places, things, and people to which we say or do it.

Taking some time out of every day to reflect on the events of the day, helps us focus on what we intended to say or do. We all develop our own routines of daily living. These routines become habits that we use to see and relate to the world around us. We travel to work every day without always consciously thinking about it. We groom and dress ourselves with whatever is available that day with little conscious thought. We practice general hygiene, brushing our teeth when we arise and before going to bed, and perhaps even flossing every day, because that's what we've always done.

A certain amount of routine behavior is necessary to operate in the world. However, it is also very easy to become locked into behaviors, losing all thought of why we are doing certain things or if changes should occur after a period of doing the same things or always doing them the same way. Dressing without much forethought is a different context than thinking intentionally about how you want to present to the world for that day or occasion. Brushing and flossing are necessary habits, but doing it because you always have is very different from brushing and flossing as an act of good health and hygiene.

Most of us drive to work, travelling the same route every day. While this might be useful and feels comfortable, relating to our partners or our children in an automatic way is similarly disconnected in impact. It takes us away from the moment that is unfolding. This kind of unconscious behavior allows us to be physically present but not really showing up. We can all think of some days where we go through the motions without consciously thinking about the why's of it or the possible consequences of such routine behaviors.

In order to become more aware of our thoughts and actions and their impacts on us and others, the practice of conscious intention can be a vital point of departure. Living your life with conscious intention is an act of awakening –like flying manually, not on autopilot. This practice is worth adopting, if only on the smallest level—in daily minute-by-minute interactions —as well as on a larger, higher level of planning for the kind of life you value. Conscious intention can help you chart a future for yourself, which will benefit your physical, mental, spiritual, and emotional selves as well as the world we all live in.

A large portion of this book focuses on the list of key behaviors and actions to be considered in living your life with conscious intention. They should help you think about how you approach your interactions with yourself and others in your work, home, community, church, and the world as a whole. My conscious intention is to encourage you to become more aware of these things as you proceed through each and every day for the rest of your life.

Note that this list is in no way exhaustive. There are far more words and phrases which can be used to reflect conscious intention. However, this list is important to me and others with whom I have shared it. Making a serious and earnest effort to consider these in my life helps me know I am making a difference and the world could be a better place for this.

I have also "sprinkled" some of my original poetry throughout my discussions of these key behaviors and actions. As always, I enjoy sharing them and I hope you find some support and inspiration from those I have included.

Let this book help you assess your current beliefs and paradigms on being consciously intent to ensure their currency and validity. Over the years, we become comfortable with things deposited in our brains, by both ourselves and others, and we miss the numerous opportunities to re-evaluate them throughout our lives.

As you read through the key behaviors, you will, more than likely, come up with your own additions to the list. If that's the case, then I will have accomplished more than I set out to. Feel free to let me know.

"Awakening to the true state of our world can only happen when we awaken to the true state of ourselves. We can heal the outer world only by healing our inner world." — Unknown

Chapter 2
Conscious Intention
Is A Choice

"Intention is living day to day, even moment to moment, with a sense of conscious choice. It means being continuously conscious of how those choices, as a result of our conscious intention, relate to our values and goals–and where there are the greatest opportunities to make a difference in our lives and those of others." — Unknown

As with any change, you must *choose* to live a life of conscious intention. This involves giving up certain unproductive habits and practices, and assuming some new ones. In order to determine what needs to go and what can stay, you will have to assess how successful and satisfied you are with your current behaviors and way of life. Ask yourself these key questions (self-honesty is important). Your responce can be "Always", "Sometimes", or "Never". This list is not exhaustive but represents a sampling of key behaviors or attitudes of which you should become more aware in order to strive toward a more conscious intention.

Do I tend to dwell on the negative?
Do I have unwarranted envy of others or for things I wish I had?
Do I harbor ill feelings toward others for no apparent or justifiable reason?
Do I speak harshly to others when kind words are more appropriate?
Do I speak ill of others when they are not present?

Do I look to others for my happiness and satisfaction?

Do I tend to stretch, hide, omit, or otherwise taint the truth?

Do I avoid opportunities to be helpful to others?

Do I tend to overreact to simple situations or comments?

Do I tend to allow distractions when I should be listening?

Do I tend to be too quick to judge others?

Do I tend to neglect or avoid responsibility for my actions and behaviors?

Do I act on impulse before thinking about the impact on others or myself?

Do I expect from others what I am not willing to give?

Do I wonder what my true purpose is in life?

If you honestly answered "Always" or "Sometimes" to any one or more of these questions, conscious intention may be something you wish to choose to pursue. If you chose "Never" to all of the questions, this book may not be for you. You may already be living with conscious intention. However, keep in mind that we all have a tendency toward some of these behaviors, at least sometimes.

If you feel you may gain better insight into your behaviors and how they relate to conscious intention, please read on. Conscious Intention can help you gain better control of your actions and improve outcomes. It can help you relate better to others. You may see how improvements can be made in your life because you see where they are needed. With conscious intention, you remain aware of the world around you and there are fewer surprises in your life.

You must choose different behaviors before you will effectively engage in them.

You must be committed to working through the changes required with the choice and, if you stick to it, you will change the way you perceive your life and the purpose for which you were placed here on this earth.

CHOICE LEADS TO CHANGE

It's not easy but, if you make the choice, you must make the change. Change requires taking control of your life. You will stop being a victim of your past and start moving on to something new and more fulfilling.

It may be uncomfortable at first. As with most change, adjustments must be made. God gets us through what He wants us to go through. Therefore, change also requires trust in God — that He will lead us to the end result He has already charted for our lives.

The choice is always yours.

"When you have to make a choice and don't make it, that is in itself a choice." —William James

Quotes on Making Choices

"Life is a sum of all your choices"
— Albert Camus

"Your life is the sum result of all the choices you make, both consciously and unconsciously. If you can control the process of choosing, you can take control of all aspects of your life. You can find the freedom that comes from being in charge of yourself."   — Robert F. Bennett

"It is our choices ... that show what we truly are, far more than our abilities."
— Anonymous

"One's philosophy is not best expressed in words; it is expressed in the choices one makes. In the long run, we shape our lives and we shape ourselves. The process never ends until we die. And, the choices we make are ultimately our own responsibility."
— Eleanor Roosevelt

Chapter 3
Conscious Intention Must Be Practiced

Practice is 1) repeated exercise in or performance of an activity or skill so as to acquire or maintain proficiency; 2) the actual application or use of an idea, belief, or method, as opposed to theories relating to it. — Oxford Dictionary

If you are to become better and more effective at anything you pursue, you must practice. This requires time, discipline, commitment, and sometimes sacrifices. Some examples include *continuous learning, healthy living,* and *spirituality*. These and many other activities must be practiced in order to make them truly internal to your being. Practice requires a conscious effort to achieve what you intend to.

If you choose to live a *healthy life*, you must make more conscious and intentional choices about your eating, exercising, doctor visits, relaxation, and rest. You must develop a practice of becoming aware of everything you eat or drink and how it can impact your health, positively or negatively. You must develop a schedule of regular exercise and set goals for accomplishing your weight and fitness objectives. You must visit your doctor regularly, as needed, and follow his/her instructions and prescriptions.

If you choose to lead a more *spirit-centered life*, you must practice praying, reading and understanding the Bible, devotionals, and other spiritual works. You must worship and serve a higher being than yourself, and make every effort to get closer to Him.

You must practice giving and sharing and paying more attention to others in need of your gifts and talents.

Continuous learning requires not only a desire to gain more knowledge in areas that interest you, and that you can apply to assist others, but to actively pursue and practice that desire. This can be accomplished through reading a variety of books and publications, taking courses — either classroom or electronic — practicing more attentive listening skills in meetings and personal conversations, and taking advantage of any opportunity to learn more.

I have read dozens of books on topics such as living in the "now" or being present, how relationships should work, inspiring and helping others, improving spiritual awareness, faith and hope, paying attention, and many other motivational topics for enriching and living a purposeful life. The common thread in all these books, as well as the two I have written previously, involves practicing the things that can make an enduring and effective difference in yourself and how you respond to those with whom you interact.

Practice helps you internalize new behaviors and causes them to become a part of your everyday living and being. It allows you to realize the change related to the choices you make to live a consciously intentional life. Anything worth doing better is worth the practice required to get there.

Think about how practice helps professionals and others to hone their craft, art, specialty, or science, such as:

- Athletes
- Lawyers

- Doctors
- Dancers
- Musicians
- Writers
- Speakers
- Actors
- Photographers
- Designers

They don't all start with expertise. It's gained and improved through practice. They try things over and over, making the necessary changes along the way, until they arrive at a comfortable place where they know they are doing the most they can do. As they move forward in life, they continue to search out opportunities and practices that allow them to get better and better. This will be the case with living a life of conscious intention.

Make conscious intention a key part of your daily life. Weave it into all your interactions, decisions, thoughts, and actions. Maintain constant awareness of what your intentions are and why. Determine if each results in the way you intend. Even if they don't, know that being aware in the first place allows you to make that determination. With practice, you'll come to realize the effectiveness of this. It should, ultimately, become a part of who you are.

**CONSCIOUS INTENTION
REQUIRES
CONSTANT PRACTICE**

Quotes on Practice

"Practice means to perform, over and over again in the face of all obstacles, some act of vision, of faith, of desire. Practice is a means of inviting the perfection desired." — Martha Graham

"We learn by practice. Whether it means to learn to dance by practicing dancing or to learn to live by practicing living, the principles are the same. One becomes, in some area, an athlete of God." — Martha Graham

"Practice is the best of all instructors." — Publilius Syrus

"An ounce of practice is worth more than tons of preaching." — Mahatma Gandhi

Chapter 4
Conscious Intention Requires Awakening

"Self-observation brings man to the realization of the necessity of self-change. And in observing himself a man notices that self-observation itself brings about certain changes in his inner processes. He begins to understand that self-observation is an instrument of self-change, a means of awakening." — George Gurdjieff

"Wake up, wake up!" Do you recall being awakened from a dream that you would rather have remained in? Or maybe you were happy to have been awakened from one where you feel you have been saved from a fate worse than death! What if you were told you exist in your own dream world, as does everyone else, all the time? And what if you could consciously control the visions and activities in your own dream and choose how, when, or even whether you want to react with the dreams of others? That would be an awakening worth pursuing!

All of us would rather spend more time in a dream where we don't ever want to leave than spending time in one where we can't wait to wake up. We have a choice. We can create the dream of our choosing by practicing conscious intention as we go through our lives here on earth.

We use an alarm clock to wake us up in the morning. It helps to have an alarm that says "Wake up, wake up!" when you are learning to practice conscious intention. One way to allow us to remain awake is to slow down and take time to digest each situation as it is presented, while paying attention to how we respond to them. Try to eliminate distractions from the "noise" surrounding your interactions, and focus on the present moment. Another way of awakening or remaining awake includes developing and maintaining an awareness of :

- What you are thinking
- Where you are
- How you are speaking and responding
- How you are feeling
- What your intentions are

The purpose of awareness is to support us in being present with the people and circumstances we are facing in the moment, rather than cogitating about the past, projecting into the future, or otherwise being carried away by sensations, feelings, thoughts, and intuitions. We develop and maintain awareness so we can reflect and respond to challenges and opportunities rather than react to them.

Awareness stems from paying attention. When someone is talking to you, do you give them your undivided attention or do you attempt to multitask? When you are reading, does your mind wander so you are not completely absorbing the message?

Splitting your attention, while sometimes necessary, becomes detrimental to your awareness and awakening when practiced more frequently than not. Just as conscious intention is a choice, you must make a choice to pay attention when someone or something requires it. If you find you are easily distracted by television, engaging music, internet surfing, routine interruptions, or other things that beg for your attention, you owe it to yourself to find ways to reduce the distractibility and choose to attend to the people and things that are most important in your life.

I mentioned 3 books in the Foreword, which deserve additional mention. If you are serious about pursuing the act of awakening in support of practicing conscious intention, you may want to take a look at those books. They are all available in both hard copy and electronic format. Again, the titles of these books are:

The Four Agreements by don Miguel Ruiz
A New Earth by Eckhart Tolle
The Book of Awakening by Mark Nepo

You may also want to check out *The Fifth Agreement*, also by don Miguel Ruiz, which includes a recap of *The Four Agreements*, while providing additional insight into relationships (*The Four Agreements* focused more on personal behaviors).

Quotes on Awakening/Awareness

"It is not until you awaken and become fully present that you will realize that you have not been present. It is not until you awaken that you will realize you have been asleep, dreaming that you are awake."   — Leonard Jacobson

"Awareness is the greatest agent for change."
— Eckhart Tolle

"What is necessary to change a person is to change his awareness of himself."
— Abraham Maslow

"The purpose of our lives is to give birth to the best that is in us. It is only through our own personal awakening that the world can be awakened. We cannot give what we do not have."   — Marianne Williamson

Chapter 5
Conscious Intention Activities

"The field of consciousness is tiny. It accepts only one problem at a time."   *– Antoine de Saint-Exupery*

There are a number of activities in life involving or requiring conscious intention, including:

- Listening
- Speaking
- Reading
- Writing
- Driving

This is just a small sample, but it should give you a basic idea of how you approach some of life's activities that are common to us all. In her book, *The Power of Inner Choice: 12 Weeks to Living a Life YOU Love*, Mary E. Allen provides specific activities allowing you to practice living in the present as opposed to the past or future. She includes topics and exercises on areas such as Getting Connected, Visioning from the Inside Out, Aligning Energetically, and Conscious Choice.

To practice conscious intention with these activities, I have included some suggestions on how to bring yourself into the present. I am by no means an expert. However, I have tried them and feel they are worth trying for yourself. These suggestions can result in success, if you are willing to approach them with that attitude.

Listening

You can determine if this is an area which requires more conscious intention by paying more attention to whether or not you practice the following:

- Interrupting or talking while someone else is talking
- Being unresponsive when someone is attempting to engage you in conservation
- Not bothering to ask questions for clarification
- Attending to other things, like watching television, surfing the internet, listening to music, or other distracting activities, while someone is conversing with you

Once you become aware that you may be practicing such behaviors, you can improve by maintaining this awareness. Considering our reasons for listening, including obtaining information and understanding, learning, improving relationships, gaining respect and reciprocity, and for enjoyment, we have much to gain by trying this out.

Good listening skills require keen self-awareness. If you understand your own personal style of listening, that will go a long way in creating good and lasting impressions with others.

Speaking

Just as important as how you listen is how you speak — so people will listen. You should be aware of your speaking habits and approach them with conscious intention. Here are some ways you can determine if you are speaking with self-awareness and effectiveness:

- Others tend to correct your grammar while you are speaking
- Others interrupt you when you are speaking
- You find it difficult to hold the attention of others while you are speaking
- You give in to distraction while you are speaking (you interrupt yourself)
- You make constant apologies when speaking
- You use "fillers" like Ah, Um, You know, and Er
- You have to search for words
- You speak as though you know more than you actually do

These habits can affect how your listeners relate to you or cause them to avoid having to listen to you. If you determine you are affected by such behaviors, either on your part or that of your listeners, continue to maintain this awareness with all interactions and conversations. To do this, try actively listening to yourself when you speak. Concentrate on your tone, choice of words, the message you are trying to provide, the reason you are speaking, and the results you expect to gain. Check the body language of your listeners to determine if they are receiving the message in the manner and intent you are delivering it. If the message is not accepted as intended, take a pause before responding or trying to clarify. This will allow you to think about your response before providing it, while trying to ensure you properly engage the listener to receive their intended response.

Reading

In order to determine if you are reading with conscious intention, you can test yourself. Share what you've read with others and see how well you remember the content and the message. If you seem to have trouble remembering what you read, ask these questions:

- Are there any distractions?
- Am I interested in what I am reading?
- Do I have more pressing issues to think about?
- Am I paying attention to what I am reading?
- Am I making notes to help remember or reference what I am reading?
- Am I learning anything from my reading?

If any of these apply, determine how you can address that particular issue. If you can't get rid of the distractions and you can't read through them, try reading when they are not an issue. If you are reading something that does not interest you, unless it is required, choose something more interesting. Try paying closer attention to what you are reading and take some notes to jog your memory when you decide to apply what you learn. Try scheduling your reading time when you are more apt to pay closest attention to the content. If you're going to read, clear everything else away, so you have nothing but you and the book or reading material.

Again, maintaining self-awareness of what helps you live with conscious intention will go a long way in arriving and remaining in this state.

Writing

Whether you're writing a letter or a note, making a list, or working toward publishing an article or book, your actions require conscious intention to be effective. Paying attention to your writing involves concentration and focus. You also need to ensure you proofread your writing to avoid costly or embarrassing mistakes. Writing with conscious intention makes your words more meaningful to your readers.

Rushed writing, without conscious intention, frequently results in an inferior product.

Driving

Data from the National Highway Traffic Safety Administration (NHTSA) shows that in 2008 almost 6,000 people died in crashes involving reports of distracted driving, and an estimated 20 percent of all crashes on U.S. roadways involved distracted driving.

Distracted driving is any activity that could divert a person's attention away from the primary task of driving. All distractions endanger driver, passenger, and bystander safety. These types of distractions include:

- Texting
- Using a cell phone or smartphone
- Eating and drinking
- Talking to passengers
- Grooming
- Reading, including maps
- Using a navigation system
- Watching a video
- Adjusting a radio, CD player, or MP3 player

Because text messaging requires visual, manual, and cognitive attention from the driver, it is by far the most alarming distraction.

Facts and Statistics on the consequences and dangers of driving without conscious intention:

- In 2009, 5,474 people were killed in crashes involving driver distraction, and an estimated 448,000 were injured. (NHTSA)

- 16% of fatal crashes in 2009 involved reports of distracted driving. (NHTSA)

- 20% of injury crashes in 2009 involved reports of distracted driving. (NHTSA)

- In the month of June 2011, more than 196 billion text messages were sent or received in the US, up nearly 50% from June 2009. (CTIA)

- Teen drivers are more likely than other age groups to be involved in a fatal crash where distraction is reported. In 2009, 16% of teen drivers involved in a fatal crash were reported to have been distracted. (NHTSA)

- 40% of all American teens say they have been in a car when the driver used a cell phone in a way that put people in danger. (Pew)

- Drivers who use hand-held devices are 4 times more likely to get into crashes serious enough to injure themselves. (Monash University)

- Text messaging creates a crash risk 23 times worse than driving while not distracted. (VTTI)

- Sending or receiving a text takes a driver's eyes from the road for an average of 4.6 seconds, the equivalent — at 55 mph — of driving the length of an entire football field, blind. (VTTI)

- Headset cell phone use is not substantially safer than hand-held use. (VTTI)

- Using a cell phone while driving — whether it's hand-held or hands-free — delays a driver's reactions as much as having a blood alcohol concentration at the legal limit of .08 percent. (University of Utah)

- Driving while using a cell phone reduces the amount of brain activity associated with driving by 37%. (Carnegie Mellon)

    As you make a choice to pursue and practice more conscious intention, try to keep these statistics in mind. Also, think about other activities you engage in where you can benefit from conscious intention. You owe it to yourself, your friends, co-workers, family, and even strangers to become more aware of all activities and interactions requiring your attention.

Abbreviations:

- CTIA — Cellular Telephone Industries Association
- NHTSA — National Highway Traffic Safety Administration
- Pew — Pew Research Center
- VTTI — Virginia Tech Transportation Institute

Quotes on Conscious Intention Activities

"The most basic of all human needs is the need to understand and be understood. The best way to understand people is to listen to them."
— Ralph Nichols

"Success demands singleness of purpose."
— Vince Lombardi

"Life is denied by lack of attention, whether it be to cleaning windows or trying to write a masterpiece." — Nadia Boulanger

"Writing must always have intention because words have power." — Suheir Hammad

Part II:
Key Behaviors For Enriching Our Lives

On the following pages, I have compiled seventy-four behaviors which I consider key in our quest toward living a life of conscious intention. Each one includes a discussion on what it means and how it can be applied to improve our quality of life as well as that of others. While all of them may not apply to you or your particular state of being, you may find that at least some of them do. I encourage you to take some time to read through them all and see how they can be used to improve your efforts toward awakening to a better way of interacting with yourself, God, and others.

*If something doesn't turn out like
You thought it might or should
Don't dwell on it, but learn a thing
See both the bad and good.*

1. Be Accepting

To accept means to receive as adequate, valid, or suitable. This speaks to the importance of accepting yourself and others, as well as your current status in life, and all things God has seen fit to provide for and to you.

Accepting yourself means you know who you are or who you can become. You are not easily swayed away from this center. You believe God has placed you in this life for a purpose and He will take you through the process of fulfilling it. You refrain from damaging self-judgment.

Accepting others extends to or from acceptance of yourself, and allows you to treat them with the love and kindness God meant for you and them. This means you are consciously aware of the importance of all life and you do not engage in judging others for who you think they should be or what you think they should do.

Accepting your current status in life, however sufficient or insufficient you perceive it to be, gives you the ability and incentive to either plan to do better when you need to or ensure you are grateful for what you have been given. It shows you know that He is in control.

Open your mind and heart to situations and opportunities to be accepting. When you see and value the differences between you and others, in their cultures and habits, in their views and practices, you can begin to accept them as well as you accept yourself.

2. Be Accommodating.

Put Others First

*"Do the right thing."
Is easy to say,
If you are the one who is
Getting your way.*

*It may be harder
And harder to do
If the winner of the struggle
Is other than you.*

*Looking past yourself, you see
Is what's called for with this.
Thinking of others surely could be
What is first on your list.*

*When you become tempted
To always put yourself first
Try thinking, praying,
Or reading a verse,*

*From God's great collection
Of how we should live.
It's the ultimate guide
Which makes it easier to give.*

The definition of accommodating is:

- helpful in bringing about a harmonious adaptation
- Obliging; willing to do favors

Being accommodating reflects a certain sensitivity to the feelings and needs of others. It encourages you to be supportive, kind, and nurturing. If you are accommodating, you are more ready to cooperate and you may believe in the old adages, "you catch more flies with honey than you do with vinegar" or "it is better to give than to receive".

Being accommodating does not mean neglecting your own needs and desires just to constantly please others, to be accepted by them, or to the detriment of your own best interest. It does not mean allowing others to take advantage of your kindness and support.

Try not to view situations as an inconvenience when others require your understanding or assistance. Be accommodating but without surrendering your own valid convictions. There will be instances where being accommodating may not be best in a particular situation or in the best interest of others. As you become more self-aware and develop your own personal level of conscious intention, you will be able to better determine and distinguish between these instances.

3. Be Accountable.

Accountability extends across all areas of life, both personal and professional. Being accountable means you are willing to accept the responsibility and consequences of your actions and decisions. This includes commitments you endeavor and plans you pursue. It includes promises you make to yourself and others, as well as any judgment calls you choose to chance. It applies to relationships, health, spirituality, education, careers, and all of life's pursuits.

Being accountable means you refrain from making excuses for your failures and areas you sometimes neglect. It means you choose not to blame others for these failures and neglect or for your mistakes or shortcomings. In this position, you understand decisions of others to hold you accountable, whenever warranted.

Holding yourself accountable requires being honest with yourself. This can empower you to move forward with your life and all that awaits you in your future. It encourages you to live life with integrity and honesty, admitting to yourself when you err, swallowing your pride, and apologizing to others when needed.

"It is easy to dodge our responsibilities, but we cannot dodge the consequences of dodging our responsibilities." — Sir Josiah Stamp

"You are accountable for your actions, your decisions, your life; no one else is, but you." — Catherine Pulsifer

"Life is not accountable to us. We are accountable to life."
— Denis Waitley

"Appreciation can make a day – even change a life. Your willingness to put it into words is all that is necessary."   — Margaret Cousins

"The deepest principle in human nature is the craving to be appreciated."
— William James

---

4. Show Appreciation.

"I consider my ability to arouse enthusiasm among men the greatest asset I possess. The way to develop the best that is in a man is by appreciation and encouragement."   — Charles Schwab

You can show appreciation either by simply saying "Thank you", or you can take some action to let others know you appreciate them or something they have done. There are many, many ways to show appreciation. Here are just a few:

- Gift-giving
- Lending a hand
- Treating someone to a meal, a show, or other outing
- Giving a hug
- A pat on the back
- Sending a note indicating appreciation
- Sending flowers
- Writing or giving a poem or meaningful poetry

Showing appreciation adds value to relationships and lets the recipient know you truly care. When you align your words with actions, it adds credibility to you as an individual and you are viewed as being sincere.

Showing appreciation can result in reciprocity—when someone knows you appreciate them, generally they will, in turn, appreciate you.

Show appreciation regularly and always be sincere. Yet you should not always expect that others will show appreciation as you do or as you would like them to.

If you have been the recipient of appreciation more often than you tend to give it, check to see if this is your conscious intention.

"My son, pay attention to my wisdom, turn your ear to my words of insight." — *Proverbs 5:1*

5. Give Attention.

Attention: *the act or state of applying the mind to something; a condition of readiness for such attention involving especially a selective narrowing or focusing of consciousness and receptivity.*

Show others you care by "giving" them your attention when they are trying to engage you in activities, conversation, or other experiences. This idea is a little more than just "paying" attention. Giving attention involves making yourself fully available to others not just by listening to what they say and responding to them but also making them feel they are the only object of your attention at any given moment. You eliminate all other distractions in favor of attention to the matter at hand.

Giving your spouse attention may mean taking them out, buying them something special, complimenting them, and letting them know how much you appreciate them.

Giving attention to your children could be reflected in simple acts of spending uninterrupted time with them and showing them you are interested in their accomplishments and talents.

Occasional phone calls, emails, or printed notes give your attention to friends and family to let them know you are thinking about them.

Giving attention to yourself and the things you want to accomplish in life should not be neglected.

Be consciously aware of what matters to you as well as to others.

6. Maintain Balance.

Maintaining balance in your life includes the four dimensions I referred to in my book, *Pay Attention To Your Life*. If you think of your life in this manner, and pay attention to balancing these dimensions, they become key to a more fulfilling life. These areas include the following:

Mental — This reflects how we think about our life, the beliefs we hold, as well as our conscious and subconscious thoughts. What we think in our minds determines largely what we will or have become, how we behave, and the way we set and achieve our goals in life. The mind is where we maintain a relationship with ourselves.

Physical — pertains to the care and feeding of our body and includes our basic needs for nutrition, exercise, relaxation, and rest. This is our temple—the home we have been given to live in while on earth.

Emotional — reflects the heart of our being—the center of our emotions and feelings toward ourselves and others. This is where our attitudes are created or influenced. Love, anger, fear, happiness, and sadness are all examples of our emotions.

Spiritual — refers to the soul which is a non-physical entity capable of perception and self-awareness. The dictionary defines it as an attitude or principle that inspires, animates, or pervades thought, feeling, or action.

Paying attention to these areas promotes a balanced existence. We must pay attention to them all to maintain this balance. When we neglect one or more areas, the others will suffer. Each part is directly related to the others, which links the needs of one part to the needs of the whole person.

7. Believe In something.

Life's Purpose

If I can know I've changed the world
In some small means or measure;
And others see my constant efforts
As a legacy to treasure;

I'll know I've served a purposeful life
That the Good Lord so intended;
And when I leave this earthly existence
No one will have to defend it.

Think of me as one more soul
Who saw the message clearly;
And reached out most faithfully
To touch each heart so dearly.

Try to find a Point of Light
Shining brightly on your good deeds,
As one of God's most special ones
Reaching out to those with needs.

When you believe in something, even if it's only yourself, life becomes worth living. You are no longer just existing, you are alive and have things to look forward to.

No one can tell you what to believe in. Only you can make that determination and choice. People believe in different things, for different reasons. Most believe in a power or existence higher than themselves. Others believe in material accomplishments or acquisitions. Some believe in a secure future, family, career, love, social responsibility, or justice. Most of us believe in both good and evil and a clear difference between right and wrong. The majority of us believe in all of these as well as many other things.

Our beliefs can lift us up and provide a certain level of comfort. There are so many things we can believe in and, if we look around, with conscious intention, we are bound to find what is waiting for us.

Once you determine what to believe in, you must then act on it to ensure it becomes a part of your purpose and you realize its value to your life.

"A man lives by believing something: not by debating and arguing about many things."   *— Thomas Carlyle*

"Believing in who you are is a major part of a powerful combination for success.   *— Darren L. Johnson*

"To succeed you have to believe in something with such a passion that it becomes a reality."   *— Anita Roddick*

8. Get Better.

If you become too content with who you are or where you are in life, you may lack incentive or motivation to improve or get better. Additionally, if you don't know who you are or what your purpose is in life, you have little motivation to change.

There is always room to get better, be it mentally, physically, emotionally, or spiritually. In doing so, you not only benefit yourself, but others around you.

We all have strengths and weaknesses. We can capitalize on those strengths but that won't always compensate for the weaknesses. Knowing ourselves and the areas where we are not strong, gives us that starting point. Sometimes this may not feel comfortable to admit to and address these areas; however, if we choose to get better, a conscious awareness of where and how we can get better, and the rewards of doing so, will boost confidence and move us further toward a more fulfilling life.

Getting better may take courage and with God's help, we can succeed. Try assessing areas of your life where you can get better in order to enhance your life experiences. Become a better speaker, writer, parent, employee, friend, or spouse, or just do a better job of helping and supporting others.

"Be anxious for nothing, but in everything by prayer and supplication with thanksgiving let your requests be made known to God."
— Philippians 4:6

"Growth begins when we begin to accept our own weakness."
— Jean Vanier

9. Observe Boundaries.

Boundaries

*Boundaries are necessary
To keep our kids from harm.
We set them up like sand-to-sea
So they feel safe and warm.*

*They may roar and may rebel
But we must stand steadfast.
The lessons we teach today
Are truly the ones that last.*

*Boundaries are also set
To keep us in our place,
And help us know the way to go
In returning to our base.*

*We sometimes try to reach beyond
The line He drew for us;
And He is there to let us know
That all we need is trust.*

*Sometimes He may allow us
To stretch beyond that line;
This only serves to help us see
His truth is most divine.*

*For when the right time comes along
To move beyond His mark
We will know the journey upon which
He leads us to embark.*

We all have boundaries in our lives that we should not cross. They must be observed for the protection of ourselves, our loved ones, and others.

Boundaries exist in conversations, relationships, workplace interactions, and many other areas. Boundaries can be personal or professional, physical or emotional, mental or spiritual. Knowing how far to go without offending others, or overstepping your boundaries and resulting in unintended outcomes or consequences, is worth noting.

Boundaries may be set by you, others with whom you interact, the government, and God. In order to observe these limits, you must become aware of them, either through direct or indirect interaction, researching, or simply asking. This relates to your conscious intention in determining and setting boundaries. This may also allow mutual re-setting or elimination of existing boundaries.

Some boundaries may be set to restrict and some are set to protect. Either way, ignoring them could be detrimental.

Failure to observe or respect boundaries set by you or others, may imply or indicate you don't care about them or that you are behaving without conscious intention.

10. Stay Calm.

"People look at me and see a calm, cool guy on the sidelines and I want them to know that my Christian faith affects my coaching and everything I do." — *Tony Dungy*

Staying calm is called for in many different situations. Among them are times when things don't seem to go as planned. You may be having a good day that suddenly goes bad. You may have been in an accident that wasn't your fault. You may have an altercation with a spouse, co-worker, sibling, or child. You may end up in a state of confusion, panic, or even heated by anger. Losing your cool won't help much in getting you out of such situations. It can only make things worse. It's important to stay calm so you can assess the situation properly and take the appropriate actions. Try remembering that you can work things out as long as you exercise conscious intention.

There are a number of things you can do to stay calm in these and other irritating situations. Choose the ones that may work for you. Some can be applied in the midst of a situation while others work best after or to head it off before it gets there.

- Take a few deep breaths
- Remove yourself from the situation, temporarily
- Settle down with a cup of coffee or tea
- Meditate and pray about it
- Be present; maintain awareness of your behavior
- Listen to soothing music
- Read a good book
- Exercise
- Take a walk

You owe it to yourself for health, good relationships, and success in life to stay calm as much as possible.

11. Provide Clear Expectations.

Whether you're dealing with your spouse, children, co-workers, community, or superiors, you must be clear about what is expected of them and yourself. Regardless of the situation, providing clear expectations ensures the best chance of a successful outcome.

Making assumptions about whether or not others understand what you expect without being clear, can result in frustration, conflicts, and other ill feelings on both sides. Additionally, don't make others guess what your expectations are. Giving clear expectations allows others a means of assessing if they hit or miss the mark.

In many cases, it helps to put things in writing and have a discussion about them. Ask for feedback to ensure it's understood.

Providing clear expectations may involve identifying timing, quality, quantity, level of completion, cost, size, and other attributes desired or required. Be sure to determine if your expectations are realistic and can be met in these areas before you make a request.

Always explain, in detail, what you expect. Communicate what you perceive the different roles are for a specific project, task, or experience. Don't leave anyone guessing as to what your expected outcomes are. Be patient as others try to accommodate your expectations and demands.

12. Be Committed.

Commitment

*Commit yourself to the things in your life
And don't fear going the distance.
Keep your mind ever focused and ready
And never lose your persistence.*

*Stick with your goals and don't let them go.
Keep moving ever forward and then you will know
Commitment requires that you weather some storms
Many ups and downs outside of life's norms.*

*As long as you have faith
Keeping God as your guide,
You won't fear risking failure -
As you keep a constant stride.*

"Commit your work to the Lord., then it will succeed."
— *Proverbs 16:3*

For the things you are determined to accomplish in life, you must be committed to ensure the best chance of succeeding. The formal definition of commitment is:

- an agreement or pledge to do something in the future
- the state or an instance of being obligated or emotionally impelled

By being committed to a particular endeavor, you make an agreement with yourself and others to see it through. You feel obligated or impelled to carry it out with the best efforts you can bring.

Commitment covers a lot of areas in life. You can be committed to finding and fulfilling your purpose in life. You must be committed to your marriage or personal relationships, career, family and friends, caring for others, and many other pursuits where you would like to succeed.

We can be committed to living our lives with conscious intention by following any of these key behaviors, practices, and corresponding activities identified while paying closer attention to how we move through each day.

"The quality of a person's life is in direct proportion to their commitment to excellence, regardless of their chosen field of endeavor."   — *Vince Lombardi*

"There's a difference between interest and commitment. When you're interested in doing something, you do it only when circumstance permit. When you're committed to something, you accept no excuses, only results."   — *Unknown*

Compassion: *a feeling of deep sympathy and sorrow for another who is stricken by misfortune, accompanied by a strong desire to alleviate the suffering.*

13. Show Compassion.

When you show compassion, you are indicating that you care about adverse experiences others may be having and your desire to help make things better. In most cases, this is basic human nature. When you are conscious of your intention to help another through such an experience, you understand what this means.

Showing compassion goes further than sympathy or empathy. When you show compassion, you also have a desire to take some action to eliminate the suffering another is experiencing.

Showing compassion involves good listening skills, an open heart, and acts of kindness, shown without expecting anything in return. When you can relate, in some way, on some level, to what someone is going through, your act of compassion is more genuine than if you simply feigned understanding.

The satisfaction we get by showing compassion can increase our own feelings of self-worth and happiness. Knowing we are providing comfort and relief for others is what humanity is based on.

Showing compassion allows us to be true to our own spirituality and the teachings in the Bible, including the Good Samaritan, the rescue of baby Moses, the freedom of the Israelites, the death and life of His son Jesus Christ, and many, many other instances.

"If you want others to be happy, practice compassion. If you want to be happy, practice compassion."   — *Dalai Lama*

"If you stop learning, you stop creating history and become history."
— *Vadim Kotelnikov*

14. Engage In Continuous Learning.

Continuous learning enables continuous growth in whatever area you choose. Our world is changing every day and there are new things to explore and learn all the time. Current knowledge and specific skills can become obsolete as time passes. Without continuous learning, we could be left behind.

Engage in continuous learning through reading, training, writing, research, communication with others, college courses, and any other avenues you have at your disposal.

It doesn't matter what your formal education level is, you can always engage in continuous learning — not so much to gain formal credentials (which is good to do), but to gain more wisdom and knowledge to pursue your life's purpose and dreams you set for yourself and others.

Continuous learning can provide the knowledge and skills to help bridge the gap between where you are and where you want to go. To do this, you have to learn and practice new skills and abilities along with new attitudes and methods, as well as some new techniques and practices.

Continuous learning allows you to get more out of yourself as well as those with whom you interact. It promotes success, confidence, and a sense of well-being.

"It's what you learn after you know it all that counts."
— *Harry S. Truman*

"Be devoted to one another in brotherly love. Honor one another above yourselves." — Romans 12:10

15. Be Devoted.

When you are devoted to someone or something, you show loyalty and commitment. You focus on their well-being or successful outcome. You tend to feel or display strong affection or attachment for that or those to which you are devoted.

If you walk in faith, your devotion to God and your spirituality is first and foremost evident. You can also be devoted to a number of people in your life, including your spouse, children, family members, co-workers, church members, and others.

Career, health, and your true purpose in life could also be on your list of things to which you are devoted. I'm sure you can come up with others.

Being devoted gives you something to hold onto and look forward to. It allows you to focus on the success of someone other than yourself or things that matter only to you. In doing so, you allow our heavenly Father to take care of your needs while "you honor one another above yourselves." (Roman 12:10)

Assess your inventory of things and people receiving your devotion and ensure they are all positive. Being devoted to something or someone who exhibits negative tendencies or behavior could be detrimental to you, those you care for, or the things that have particular meaning in your life.

Exercise conscious intention to ensure you properly direct your devotion.

16. Value Diversity.

A President for All of America

*We may never have been so full of pride
As what we are feeling tonight.
America has cast an important vote
And, yes we got it right!*

*A President for all of us
Is all we've ever wanted.
A man after our own beliefs –
A loyal American – undaunted.*

*We have a duty as Americans
To respect and not impede.
We have a responsibility
To support and follow his lead.*

*President-elect Obama we salute you
With our hands and within our hearts,
And pledge to you right here, right now,
In earnest to do our parts.*

*Success to you on the road ahead,
Good Luck, Godspeed, All the Best.
We stand behind you with strong support
And loyalty – whatever the test!*

Valuing diversity allows you to understand differences while drawing on similarities to ensure equal or equitable treatment of all. Diversity exists in age, race, gender, sexual preference, religion, ethnic origin, national origin, skin color, and other attributes originating by birth or choice. Valuing diversity encourages us to eliminate our unwarranted prejudices toward these attributes when they differ from our own. Know that these attributes do not make you better or superior, only different.

Valuing diversity allows you to focus more on similarities than differences, which helps to acquire more of an appreciation for the true goodness of human nature. You are encouraged to gain a deeper understanding of people, thereby understanding yourself better. It allows you to develop new skills for relating and interacting with a wide range of people by experiencing their differences.

The world we live in is diverse and we cannot change that. In order to exist in harmony, as God intended, we must value all of His children, not just ourselves or those who are similar to us.

"We all should know that diversity makes for a rich tapestry, and we must understand that all the threads of the tapestry are equal in value no matter what their color."   *— Maya Angelou*

"I have a dream that my four children will one day live in a nation where they will not be judged by the color of their skin, but by the content of their character."   *— Dr. Martin Luther King, Jr.*

17. Follow Your Dreams.

The Columbia Seven

They were people just like us
Who had a dream for life.
Endeavors they all knew would help
To save our World from strife.

Their reach was so much higher than
Any imaginable grasp.
So far beyond the skies unknown
And such a formidable task.

They left behind sad families
To grieve and hold them dear.
Who also know, within their hearts
That their loved-ones are always near.

What inspiration can we take
From these seven brave souls?
We must find hope and fortitude
As our own dream unfolds.

Kalpana, David, Laurel, Michael,
William, Rick, Ilan –
You're remembered in our hearts and minds
As you explore the greatest beyond.

"Hold fast to dreams, for if dreams die, life is a broken winged bird that cannot fly." — Langston Hughes

We all have dreams. I don't mean those we have while asleep. I refer to those dreams we dream while awake and conscious of what we want in life. The question is, do we follow those dreams? Or do we even know how to follow them?

Following your dreams requires conscious intention—to know what they are and to follow them without cease. A dream is not just a wish but a strong desire to be something or someone you envision yourself as.

Following your dreams means determining a path then taking the necessary steps to get there. To know what those steps are you have to set clear goals and objectives — with schedules and deadlines. Once set, you revisit your path and goals each day and assess your progress. If changes are required along the way, you will be prepared to make the necessary adjustments. As long as you keep your sights set on the final outcome, you will continue to follow your dreams until they are reached.

Be aware that there may be circumstances or individuals who discourage following your dreams, for whatever reasons. Don't let others define or try to eliminate your dreams. Expect this and be ready to address it. This may represent delays but should not cause you to abandon your dreams.

If you have dreams but don't follow them, you cheat yourself out of the life God intended for you. It's never too late to get started. Take a chance, make the effort, and go for it! You deserve it!

"Every great dream begins with a dreamer. Always remember, you have within you the strength, the patience, and the passion to reach for the stars to change the world." —Harriet Tubman

"When anger rises, think of the consequences." - Confucius

18. Show Emotional Control.

Steven Covey, in "The 7 Habits of Highly Effective People", teaches us that there is a space between stimulus and response which allows us to choose and control how we respond to the stimuli in our lives. With practice, we increase the length of the space which further allows us to improve on this habit. This relates to emotional control.

Showing emotional control requires conscious intention. It requires you to be self-aware of how you respond when stimulated, either through words or actions — internal or external.

Understand that you always have a choice in how you respond. To do this, you must know your emotions and what may or may not "set you off". There are a number of emotions common to us all, including joy, acceptance, fear, surprise, sadness, disgust, anger, and anticipation.

On a subconscious level, we may feel we are at the mercy of our emotions. By recognizing them on a conscious level, they can be better controlled. Try recognizing an emotion from the moment it presents itself and don't allow it to build or amplify. Don't ignore or constrain your feelings. This causes them to get worse and erupt later. Be aware of how you are feeling throughout the day to allow you to show better control when required to respond to some stimulus.

"Take control of your consistent emotions and begin to consciously and deliberately reshape your daily experience of life."
— Anthony Robbins

19. Embrace Life.

God's Way

*The Good Lord has His reasons
For all we do and say.
He points us in the right direction,
And leads us on our way.*

*If we complain about our life,
And ask Him why it's so,
He gently whispers His message to us
And shows us what we don't know.*

*All events throughout our lives,
Are colored with God's great pen.
He paints each chapter and every scene
From our beginning to the very end.*

*So if you question God's decisions,
Just know it'll be okay –
As long as you keep your trust in Him,
And know it's always His Way.*

Embracing life means living in the present, understanding and learning from the past, and letting the future arrive when it's time. Living with a purpose, pursuing dreams, and respecting others are some key components of embracing life. In fact, the very premise of this book, with all the key behaviors, encourage and enable us to embrace the life we have been given.

When we embrace life, we live each day as if it were our last. We learn to fear less about what will happen tomorrow and take advantage of every minute of every day.

When we embrace life, we appreciate what we have been given and don't worry about the things we don't have. We strive to get and do better and we reach out to help others do the same.

Embracing life means celebrating who we are and accepting how we are made. We focus less on our physical attributes and more on the inner, true self that defines who we really are.

Before you can embrace life, you may need to assess the things that are holding you back and eliminate them or try to address them. You may have suffered abuse, have a disability, don't consider yourself attractive, lack self-confidence, or any other negative feelings or beliefs preventing you from embracing life. Don't let this limit or stifle your desire to do and get better. There is absolutely no test, circumstance, or task that we can not overcome or get through as long we accept that God will not give us more than we can bear. You were given life. Embrace it!

"Dream as if you'll live forever, live as if you'll die today."
- *James Dean*

"Therefore encourage one another and build each other up, just as in fact you are doing." — *1 Thessalonians 5:11*

"Do not let any unwholesome talk come out of your mouths, but only what is helpful for building others up according to their needs, that it may benefit those who listen." — *Ephesians 4:29*

20. Encourage Others.

Showing encouragement to others is a means of providing positive reinforcement when they need someone to believe in them or something they want to pursue. When you encourage others, you let them know you acknowledge that what is important to them is important to you. You also let them know you are interested in what interests them.

When others speak with a gloomy attitude, rather than going along with it, listen with compassion and find a way to provide encouragement for a positive alternative.

Pursue encouragement with conscious intention. Be aware of what you are thinking and saying when an opportunity presents itself to encourage others.

Celebrate the accomplishments of others to encourage them to continue to reach higher. Let them know that in competitions, winning is not everything and you value their efforts in seeing things through.

Showing respect, praise, and acceptance of others encourages them to become more confident in you and in themselves.

Think about things that encourage you and then do those same things for others. Get to know what encourages others and give that to them. When you encourage others, you can't help but be encouraged. It's how God meant it to be for you, me, and the World.

"Personal development is your springboard to personal excellence. Ongoing, continuous, non-stop personal development literally assures you that there is no limit to what you can accomplish."
— *Brian Tracy*

21. Strive For Excellence.

Striving for excellence allows you to be or become the very best you can be. Your level of excellence may differ from that of others. You determine what that means for you. In defining your level of excellence, you must also consider all areas of your life, including physical, mental, spiritual, and emotional.

Excellence is not perfection. It requires the use of your skills, abilities, and efforts to allow you to go the extra mile in accomplishing your goals and pursuits in life.

Excellence requires you to aim higher than what currently makes you feel comfortable but not so high that you know something is clearly impossible for you to reach.

In striving for excellence, you must exercise discipline, focus, and sometimes sacrifice, while believing the final outcome will benefit not only you but others in your life or even in the world. Achieving excellence increases your self-confidence, strengthens your skills and abilities, and gives you a heightened sense of pride in your accomplishment.

Striving for excellence requires your conscious intention and attention to the details and the process needed to get there. As with everything in life, you get out of it what you put into it. In other words, "You reap what you sow". As you continue to strive for excellence, ensure you engage in continuous learning in order to continue to reach higher.

"An average plan vigorously executed is far better than a brilliant plan on which nothing is done." — Brian Tracy

22. Execute Your Plans.

In your pursuit of life's accomplishments, don't just make plans, execute them. A plan is only as good as the paper it is written on if it is not carried out.

Stephen Covey's second and third of his "7 Habits of Highly Effective People" are 'Begin with the end in mind' and 'Put first things first'. This, in essence, represents your plan (#2), and your execution (#3). Knowing where you are going gives a good start in getting there. You simply must determine what comes first and then what comes after that. Developing goals, objectives, a schedule, and milestones to execute your plan helps to keep track of progress.

As you move forward, there will be some challenges, delays, and even failures. You may become frustrated and face disappointment along the way. Conscious intention is required to help you find a way to remain motivated and adjust your plans and execution, where required, in order to keep your eye on the "prize". Anyone who has ever accomplished anything worthwhile in life has faced such obstacles. Always remember that persistence, dedication, commitment, and determination can help you succeed in defeating them and in helping to reach the desired outcome.

Make periodic and continuous assessments of your progress and celebrate your milestones to keep you interested and encouraged until you have reached your final goal. Then — move on to the next.

"Have faith in God," Jesus answered. I tell you the truth, if anyone says to this mountain, 'Go, throw yourself into the sea,' and does not doubt in his heart but believes that what he says will happen, it will be done for him. Therefore I tell you, whatever you ask for in prayer, believe that you have received it, and it will be yours. — Mark 11:22-24

23. Have Faith.

Have faith in God. Believe that He will see you through — whatever it is you're faced with. If you set goals with faith in God, He will allow success on His terms. Faith is believing in things not yet seen. You don't have to have experienced it or have seen it to know it exists or that it can happen. When you have faith, you increase the chances that what you pray or wish for will materialize. You will behave in a way that improves the chances. You will find the places that are conducive to the things you wish to achieve or accomplish.

You must keep an open mind for all the possibilities and you must believe you are deserving of what God already has in store for you. You are worthy and no one can change that. While things don't always turn out the way we want, they will always turn out the way God wants them to. That's what faith is all about.

Having faith in God means we must first believe in Him, although we cannot see Him. It is our proof that he exists.

If you have faith in God, you can have faith in yourself and all you want to accomplish. With faith in yourself, based on faith in God, you will pursue your life with the purpose given to you while taking all necessary steps and actions to realize your destiny with benefits to you and others.

"Faith is the substance of things hoped for, the evidence of things not seen." — Hebrews 11:1

24. Be Flexible.

I Believe The Lord Places Us

At times we think our life's not fair –
We pray and ask for reasons.
And wonder why we suffer so
Throughout each and every season.

The answers to our solemn prayers
Lie within our realm of trust
That through it all we realize
The Lord always places us.

I believe the Lord places us
Wherever He wants us to be
At any given place or time
Revealing what He wants us to see.

I believe the Lord places us
To accomplish His special deeds.
He lets us know, without a doubt,
He will fulfill all of our needs.

I believe the Lord places us
To experience some good and bad.
He also helps us, by His will,
To know both happy and sad.

I believe the Lord places us
Where we grow in every way –
Knowing that His hand is there
At every point throughout each day.

I believe the Lord places us
To bend but never break,
Just like the mighty palm tree
Giving us no more than we can take.

And when He's done with placing us
Down here on His green earth,
He faithfully brings us home to Him
To experience our grand re-birth.

The dictionary says you're flexible if you have "a ready capability to adapt to new, different, or changing requirements." Being flexible allows you the weigh situations and determine whether or not you need to change your position. Many times we need to adapt or adjust our way of thinking in order to encourage others to do the same. Being flexible allows us to bend but not to the point of breaking.

Standing firm, while sometimes required, may result in a no-win situation for all concerned if others are made to bend or break to satisfy your rigidity. While your firm stand may get someone else to bend, in the end, if they do it under duress, the deal will eventually fall through.

Being flexible helps in dealing with disappointments and allows you to bounce back from them more quickly. You are encouraged to find alternatives when things don't work out as you intended. When you don't find exactly what you were searching for, you have the option of either selecting something else or simply doing without it.

Learn to try different methods or take different paths when others don't work. You can still keep your eye on the prize, you just find other ways of getting there.

"Stay committed to your decisions, but stay flexible in your approach."   — Tom Robbins

"It was character that got us out of bed, commitment that moved us into action, and discipline that enabled us to follow through."
— Zig Ziglar

"As we express our gratitude, we must never forget that the highest appreciation is not to utter words, but to live by them."
— John Fitzgerald Kennedy

25. Follow Through.

If you start something, find a way to finish it. Good intentions without actions won't accomplish your goals. The world is full of individuals with good intentions. It's following through that we sometimes fail to consider.

Many of us make plans. We even write them down. Where we fail, is to determine, not only what steps to take, but to actually take those steps, ensuring they end only when we have arrived at our destination.

Following through requires action and a discipline to stick with it. Promising yourself that you will do something does not get it done. Following through is required to make it happen. Telling someone you will take an action does not ensure you will take the action. When you follow through, you actually take the action and it gets done. Don't pride yourself so much in making plans. Give yourself kudos when you realize the fruits of the labor that results from your following through.

In order to ensure you can follow through on your plans, try not to overextend yourself. This creates situations that limit your potential to follow through on all that you endeavor. While multi-tasking is desirable, it can also affect your abilities to follow through on each and every task you establish for yourself. Exercise conscious intention to ensure you remember the importance of following through.

26. Follow Up.

Follow-up involves taking the next step when you have initiated something and either delegated it to someone else, passed it on for an interim review, or you are waiting for someone else to provide input to a project, task, or other requirements you may have. It can be defined as: an action to check on or complete a previous action. Many times we pass something off to another and begin waiting for them to get back to us. Following up may be effective when you have waited a reasonable amount of time between actions. A simple text, phone call, message, or letter are all appropriate to inquire into the status. This increases the chances of effectiveness in your endeavor.

You may have submitted a resume or had a job interview. Following up may let the company or interviewer know you are truly interested and could increase your chances of landing the job or a follow-up interview.

You may have given an employee or co-worker a request for information or a task to complete. Following up with a reminder helps them know how importance it is to you and that you still require their input.

Sales people know the art of following up can improve or strengthen their customer base. They may appear too persistent, in some cases, but that's just part of their follow-up strategy. You may not need to be so persistent; however, if you want results, try following up. What do you have to lose?

"He who cannot forgive others breaks the bridge over which he must pass himself."
— George Herbert

27. Practice Forgiveness.

Practicing forgiveness is doing what God has commanded us to do. While this is true, it may not always come easy. When we find ourselves in a position of needing to forgive, we may be there because we have been offended, betrayed, or injured in some way, either physically or emotionally. In this case, we may not think the subject of our retribution deserves forgiveness. What we need to understand is that forgiveness is as much for us as for the individual who has wronged us. In some cases, the individual may not even be aware you are holding something against them. The rage or ill-feelings you carry are only affecting you. Forgiving them does not even require that you inform them, just that you, in faith, release the burden from yourself. Corrie Ten Boom, a Christian survivor of a concentration camp during the Holocaust, said, "Forgiveness is to set a prisoner free, and to realize the prisoner was you."

Forgiveness, like many things in our lives, is a choice. We can choose to remain in a state of failing to forgive, or we can do what God wants us to do and forgive. This does not mean that we forget what has happened. It means we cease letting it define who we are, what we do, and how we live our lives.

When we forgive others, according to the Bible, God will forgive us.

"Bear with each other and forgive one another if any of you has a grievance against someone. Forgive as the Lord forgave you."
— *Colossians 3:13*

Share the things you gain in life,
As you travel your appointed road.
Give generously as you receive,
And lighten your own heavy load.

28. Practice Generosity.

    Practicing generosity doesn't necessarily involve money. It can relate to being generous with your time, patience, attention, energy, good deeds, and material resources that can benefit others. Acts 20:35 tells us "It is more blessed to give than to receive." This involves giving from the heart without reservation or expectations of receiving anything in return. The Bible also tells us in 2 Corinthians 9:11, that God has given us riches for a reason: "You will be made rich in every way so that you can be generous on every occasion, and through us your generosity will result in thanksgiving to God ."

    When we practice generosity, we experience the joy of reaching out and helping those in need who could not otherwise provide for themselves. The willingness to share what God has given us lets Him know we are fulfilling our purpose in life and that we are following His instructions to us. In practicing generosity with conscious intention and an open heart, we ensure our giving is unselfish while promoting feelings of delight and happiness within ourselves.

    Practicing generosity includes tangible acts. We can think about another's situation or plight, feel empathy, kindness, or compassion, but unless these are accompanied by specific acts of giving, they won't carry the relevant depth or transformative value.

"Generosity is not giving me that which I need more than you do, but it is giving me that which you need more than I do."
                                                       — *Khalil Gibran*

29. Be Gentle.

Being gentle refers to our disposition and behavior, and it suggests a deliberate or voluntary kindness or patient endurance in dealing with others. As you develop the habit of living with conscious intention, you will become more aware of your determination to be gentle and the impact it has on both you and the recipient.

Being gentle is not always easy and sometimes requires a certain level of strength and discipline. Others may mistake your gentleness for weakness but if you are committed to being gentle, your strength will see you through. Developing better discipline and an awareness of self is key in practicing gentleness.

Being gentle involves many different aspects, including your touch, tone, speech, attitude, facial expressions and other body language, and even your spirit. When you deal with others, keep these things in mind. Many times, others respond to you based on your level or practice of gentleness.

God expects us to be gentle with everyone, including our friends, loved ones, peers, and neighbors. Living with conscious intention enables this and being aware of our words and actions can only improve our chances of success in life.

"The Lord's servant must be gentle towards all." — 2 Timothy 2:24

"A gentle answer deflects anger, but harsh words make tempers flare."   — Proverbs 15:1

30. Become Goal-oriented.

If you want to improve your chances of success in life, become goal-oriented. We all have things we wish to accomplish and sometimes we wonder why it escapes us. Why can't we just get there? The answer may just be our lack of establishing concrete goals and objectives to lead us down the appropriate path.

Once you figure out what you want to accomplish in your life, establish goals related to getting there. Then, break the goals down into objectives and define specific steps to take. Understand that you will not reach your goals overnight and you will have to stay focused as you track or monitor your progress with each step. As you complete major milestones within each goal, celebrate your success. Once the goal has been completed, give yourself due credit and begin again.

Goal-oriented individuals have a tendency toward setting and reaching specific goals. They have a strong desire to succeed in life through this process. Being goal-oriented requires determination and perseverance. While you may not succeed at every goal, this should not deter you from re-grouping and continuing to forge ahead with alternatives or new goals.

Becoming goal-oriented requires you to value the time you devote to accomplishing your goals. Allowing time for fun, relaxation, and other desired life activities should not be viewed as interference of goal accomplishment. On the contrary, these things can be considered motivation and part of the process.

31. Be Helpful.

Helping Others

When you reach out to others,
And help them in their plight,
You become a better person
In dealing with your own personal fight.

They really will appreciate
The tireless things you do,
In getting them back on a track
That eases their pain, too.

So never stop your giving
And helping others strive
To get their lives together
And continue to feel alive.

No matter what you do or say,
It's still the only way.
So reach out to another,
And fulfill your purpose today.

Being helpful involves giving or rendering aid or assistance to others in need. Opportunities to be helpful are constantly present in our lives. In some cases, help is requested and in others we volunteer without being asked. Either way, you can make a decision to reach out and help or not.

Being helpful can provide us with feelings of positive accomplishment and joyful hearts. Being helpful allows us to abide by God's commands and wishes for His children. As the Bible teaches us, when we help others, whether we know them or not, we are offering our services to God.

As you proceed throughout each day, think of ways you can be helpful, whether or not you are asked. It could be simply clearing the table after dinner, providing a blanket for warmth, taking care of the dishes, running errands, providing transportation, cooking dinner, taking out the garbage, and doing the laundry, to name a few.

When you offer comfort or condolences in times of grief, this helps family and friends bear their pain of losing someone. When you make charitable donations, you help further the cause of the institution or organization providing assistance. Offering to listen when someone needs to talk, explaining a complex subject or task, or simply being present are all ways of being helpful. The unselfish help you provide to others will always be returned to you in greater measures that you expect.

"Lies will get any man into trouble, but honesty is its own defense." — *Proverbs 12:13*

"An honest man is the noblest work of God."
— *Alexander Pope*

32. Be Honest.

"Honesty is the best policy", is something we have all heard. What this means is we should always tell the truth, no matter how much it may hurt or harm. Sometimes we think telling a "little white lie" is okay to save face or prevent another from being embarrassed or hurt. However, the truth nearly always comes out and the dishonesty will certainly be revealed, thereby threatening an otherwise good relationship.

To be honest, behave in ways that do not encourage you to have to hide the truth. This is usually a basis for not being truthful. When children behave in a way they know is not approved by parents or friends, they think lying will protect them. When couples betray a trust in a loving relationship and choose to hide it, the relationship is damaged, whether the partner knows it or not. Such dishonesty and betrayal will always loom over what could be an honest relationship between friends, co-workers, spouses, and family. If you behave in ways about which you are willing to be honest, there will be no need to lie.

Being honest needn't be harsh or filled with hurtful words or actions. You can exercise compassion in your honesty. When relationships are built on a foundation of trust and authenticity, honesty will prevail and serve the higher purpose.

"But you have an anointing from the Holy One, and all of you know the truth. I do not write to you because you do not know the truth, but because you do know it and because no lie comes from the truth." — *1 John 2:20-21*

33. Have Hope.

Hope and Faith

*Having hope is important,
Because we know that the Lord
Will preserve our faith and fortitude
As long as we do our part.*

*We must reach out to others
Giving them kindness and thought
And continue to maintain hope
That God will not leave us distraught.*

*In the face of disaster and devastation,
When things look hopeless and grim,
We wonder and cry "Why us 'O Lord!"
But we continue to have faith in Him.*

*Hope is a critical part of faith –
Praying and wishing without knowing.
If faith is believing in things not yet seen
Then hope is what keeps us going.*

*We were granted the ability to hope
So our faith could remain without waver.
Even when we don't get what we hoped for,
Our faith keeps us strong and in His favor.*

Having hope is a powerful means of sustaining our lives. It gives a reason for being. As long as we maintain hope, we have something to look forward to with confidence or expectation. Having something to look forward to gives us a reason for continuing to move forward. Having hope helps us hold on to the possibility and probability that things will turn out in a positive way.

Having hope encourages and enables us to approach life with intentional behavior that improves our chances of success. We have the feeling that what we want is within our reach and we have the courage to take the initiative to go for it.

Having hope requires we believe God has a plan for our lives and we will reach our destiny through this belief.

Having hope is more than just being optimistic. It involves establishing goals, paired with an intentional desire, and a concrete plan to achieve them.

Hope paired with faith gives us the assurance that what we expect will, in fact, occur. The hope and faith we hold are in ourselves and in God. Faith allows us to believe in things that we cannot or have not yet seen and hope keeps us expecting, with confidence, that they will be revealed to us.

"As we journey through life, the thing we long for is hope. There is no greater source of hope than God's Word." — Sandi Patty

"All of you, clothe yourselves with humility toward one another, for God opposes the proud but gives grace to the humble."
— *1 Peter 5:5*

34. Practice Humility.

Humility can be thought of as modesty in behavior, spirit, or attitude. It involves having an honest perspective of yourself. When you practice humility, you don't consider yourself any more or less important, loved, or valued by God than anyone else. You accept the gifts He has given you as well as those He has chosen to give to others. In doing so, you give Him all the credit and glory for accomplishments and achievements made by you and supported by those gifts.

When we practice humility, we do so in service to God and mankind. The Bible defines humility as the opposite of pride. Proverbs 11:2 says, "When pride comes, then comes disgrace, but with humility comes wisdom." While pride keeps us focused on ourselves instead of God, humility focuses us upon God rather than our own strengths.

When you practice humility, you refrain from a practice known as "one-upping" others, where you try to match or better any experience they may share. Humility allows you to be happy for others and not boast more about similar things you may have done.

Practicing humility does not mean you are weak, timid, or passive. You don't walk around with a bowed-head or lack confidence. Humility is derived from an acceptance through understanding our true position in the world, as a part of humanity, and a part of life. It allows us to fulfill our true purpose in life while contributing to the well-being of others.

35. Have A Sense Of Humor.

If you have a sense of humor, you are capable of being amused. You laugh at jokes and can appreciate other humorous situations. A sense of humor allows you to laugh at yourself and not be offended by things others may jokingly say about you.

Having a sense of humor helps you to dispel tension. Studies have shown that people with a well-developed sense of humor appear to be happier and healthier in life.

Having a sense of humor does not mean you laugh at every joke or are amused by dry or deprecating humor, especially when it offends you or others. Having a conscious awareness of what makes you laugh or when humor is appropriate, can increase your humor experience.

A sense of humor can enhance your family life. When you laugh together you become more connected and better able to cope with challenges. While humor is what makes something funny, a sense of humor is the ability to recognize it. Having a well-developed sense of humor helps you recognize what's funny in others and also allows you to amuse them as well.

If you have been told you don't have a sense of humor, you may not be able to appreciate different perspectives or you may take things too seriously. You may also tend to view things just on the surface and not look deeper. Try stepping out of the boundary of your comfort zone and have a good laugh.

"Imagination is the beginning of creation. You imagine what you desire, you will what you imagine and at last you create what you will."
— *George Bernard Shaw*

36. Use Your Imagination.

Imagination is defined as the act or power of forming a mental image of something not present to the senses or never before wholly perceived in reality. Using your imagination allows you to come up with creative solutions to problems and challenges in life. While we can always choose from an established collection of techniques for approaching life, imagination lets us discover or create our own. It may involve making minor adjustments or enhancements, re-inventing, or simply eliminating something altogether.

Imagination can be used in all areas of life including personal, professional, community, and educational. When you use your imagination to create what you have not yet seen or felt, it empowers you and imparts a sense of pride and confidence in what you are capable of accomplishing.

Imagination can be a powerful tool. It can be used as a negative as well as positive reinforcement. You can imagine things as not going well, and you may act in a way that causes them to manifest. However, you can do the same thing on a positive side. Imagining what you want in life and taking specific steps to obtain it, is an effective use of this quality.

"Limitations live only in our minds. But if we use our imaginations, our possibilities become limitless." — Jamie Paolinetti

"Logic will get you from A to B. Imagination will take you everywhere." — Albert Einstein

37. Show Initiative.

Don't wait to be told or asked to do something that could benefit you or others. As Nike put it, "Just do it!"

Taking or showing initiative lets you move forward with an idea, task, or other action on your own terms. It allows you to make changes that are positive and life-enriching, without waiting to be given permission to do so. It can give you the confidence you need to go further in life.

Showing initiative tells others you can act independently, without being prompted by others. While this may take courage, it also instills pride in yourself for being able to do something you may otherwise fear.

Initiative can be developed or enhanced through paying close attention to yourself, your actions, speech, and mannerisms. In other words, conscious intention is a trait that exists in this process. It requires you to know what you want to come of a situation and what your intentions are for taking the initiative.

Showing initiative follows Stephen Covey's first of the 7 Habits: Be Proactive. Following this habit allows you to take the first step toward an outcome you consciously desire and can clearly visualize. You take responsibility for your own life and make choices and initiate relative actions to follow them through. Take the initiative and take control!

38. Have Integrity.

Know what you believe in and stick to it. Know what is right and embrace it.

Having integrity means you are honest and possess strong moral principles. You stand for what is right. You show a high level of consistency in your words and actions. You practice what you preach.

When you have integrity, your actions reflect truth and honesty. Practicing integrity is an affirmation that your ideas contribute to and reflect your way of life.

When you have integrity, others see you as reliable and know they can depend on you and your decisions. They respect you for what you stand for, whether they share your beliefs or not. They know you keep your promises and you deliver on them.

Integrity is part of our moral fiber. Even if we are not born with it, it can be acquired through conscious intention by seeking out and practicing what is right. It allows you to be incorruptible, stable, consistent, and steadfast in your beliefs, values, actions, measures, and outcomes.

"Have the courage to say no. Have the courage to face the truth. Do the right thing because it is right. These are the magic keys to living your life with integrity." — *W. Clement Stone*

"In everything set them an example by doing what is good. In your teaching show integrity, seriousness." — *Titus 2:7*

39. Be Just.

In dealing with yourself and others, make decisions, choose words, and take actions that are morally right and fair.

We look to our court systems, organizations, family, and friends to treat us in a manner that is fair and equitable compared to how they treat others. They look to us to behave in the same manner. This is being just. Psalm 25:8 tells us, "God is fair and just; He corrects the misdirected, Sends them in the right direction."

If you can recall a time you were treated unjustly and how it made you feel, you understand the importance of this key behavior. Everyone deserves to be treated this way. It is our God-given right and responsibility. Isaiah 56:1 says, "Be just and fair to all," says the LORD. "Do what is right and good..."

When you practice being just, you make a statement to others that they are important and you feel more confident when you are doing what you feel is right. You are following the teachings of a higher power who treats us all in this manner.

Practice being just, with conscious intention. Know who you are dealing with, what the situation is, and how your actions and decisions impact you and others with whom you interact. Seek this trait for yourself as well as others in your life.

"He is the Rock, his works are perfect, and all his ways are just. A faithful God who does no wrong, upright and just is he."
-- Deuteronomy 32:4

40. Be Joyful.

Our Firstborn

Mommy and Daddy are very proud;
Shouting happy, shouting loud.
Took your time but finally made it;
Now we know just why you waited.

Curly hair and Daddy's mouth;
Big brown eyes and Mommy's pout;
Perfect fingers, tiny toes;
I think you've got your Mommy's nose.

A head so small and round, I see;
And little ears fit perfectly;
A smile upon your little face --
The gift of life, so full of grace.

You were sent from heaven, above
For us to have and hold and love.
We've waited very patiently,
For your arrival, finally.

And now we'll hold you in our arms;
Feel safe, sweet baby, free from harm.

    Having a joyful outlook on life can be contagious. As you interact with others throughout your life, be always willing to show joy so that others can follow your lead. Even when you are going through some trials and tribulations, there is always reason to be joyful. The fact that you are going through them and not remaining there means you are alive and there is hope. This is reason to be joyful.

    Be joyful for family and friends who share your life. Let them know that they bring you joy for being a part of your life (The poem included here was written to express our joy for our firstborn). Count and celebrate your blessings rather than dwelling on your misfortunes or failures. You can always find reason to be joyful even during the course of discouragement and sorrow.

    Be open to others who seek to help you find joy in all situations. Be open to God for giving you opportunities to find joy in whatever the situation. If you consider what you have been blessed with, this, in itself, is reason to be joyful. Simply having a roof over your head, clothes on your back, shoes on your feet, and food in your mouth is plenty. Add to that your life, regardless of any disabilities, and that God allows you to continue to be. If you opened your eyes this morning, count that as just one of the many blessing for which to be joyful.

"Be joyful always; pray continually; give thanks in all circumstances, for this is God's will for you in Christ Jesus."
                                               — 1 Thessalonians 5:16-18

41. Practice Kindness.

Kindness

Kindness costs you nothing,
Yet, it can buy more than silver, gold, or even money.

Kindness can only be given, never taken –
Once received, it becomes a torch to be passed on.

Kindness is a blanket that warms the heart.

Kindness can heal the hurt
Or ease the pain;
Soothe the soul
Or cool the flames;
Bring a smile
Or dry a tear;
Brighten a mood
Or calm a fear.

Kindness can come from stranger or friend,
Small acts or big ones, all to the same end.

You can give and receive kindness and so can I.
If more of us give it more will receive it.

Don't wait another minute,
It's simple to do
You to me, me to you.
Try a smile or lend a hand.
Give a ride or share what you can.
Kiss your kids or hug your love.
Give a wink or mend a glove.

Kindness makes a difference…

    This poem, from my first book, sums up my beliefs and feelings about practicing kindness. Reaching out to others with kind intentions fulfills God's expectations of how we live in this world with ourselves and others.

    While we may not consciously regard ourselves as being unkind, cruel, or inconsiderate, we may find instances where we were less than kind to others for whatever the reason may have been. This is not to say it was unwarranted. However, if we practice kindness in the manner intended by God, we can be assured of living in the spiritual context He meant for us.

    Consider a time or times you have been treated unkindly and how it made you feel. Now think of how your act of unkindness may make others feel. Treating someone unkind to get revenge is against what we are taught in the bible. Romans 12:19 says, "Beloved, do not avenge yourselves, but rather give place to wrath; for it is written, 'Vengeance is Mine, I will repay,' says the Lord." Further in this chapter, verse 21 tells us, "Do not be overcome by evil, but overcome evil with good."

    Practicing kindness not only allows us to feel good about ourselves. It makes others feel good and it encourages them to follow our example. Also, we are only doing what our Father has told us to do.

"Kindness is the language which the deaf can hear and the blind can see."   — *Mark Twain*

42. Listen.

Effective listening, although it may not seem so, is an active skill that requires focused attention and the avoidance of pre-forming responses until the speaker has completed the thought intended for you. You must also ensure you fully understand what is said, its intent, and the expectation of your response. Another critical practice during listening is to refrain from responding while the speaker is still speaking. As you allow the speaker to finish speaking before your respond, you also allow yourself to finish listening before you begin to speak.

Good and effective listening skills reflect your conscious intention. This ensures you are aware of what is being said to you and whether you accept or reject it. You are also aware of how it impacts you and others and allows you to maintain awareness of any intentions you have in responding regarding your understanding and your acceptance or rejection, as well as the manner in which you intend to respond.

The following quote has stuck with me over the years and contributes to my listening skills: "The complete listener is a responding listener." When you provide gestures such as nodding, smiling, or using other facial expressions and affirmations, you let the speaker know you are listening and paying attention to what is being communicated. In most one-on-one conversations, it is important to provide a response to the speaker so they know what information I received and can provide any clarification when/if needed.

"I like to listen. I have learned a great deal from listening carefully. Most people never listen."   — *Ernest Hemingway*

43. Love.

While the dictionary defines love as "an emotion of strong affection and personal attachment", it also refers to it as "a virtue representing all of human kindness, compassion, and affection" as well as "the unselfish loyal and benevolent concern for the good of another". This virtue is what I refer to when I discuss this key behavior.

Showing compassion, kindness, and affection to others, and to ourselves, is tantamount to expressing love in the human condition. It facilitates actions toward the well-being of others.

When you have love in your heart, it shows in your words and actions. You want only the best for those you care for and you are willing to sacrifice for them and their happiness.

When you love your life, you take care of yourself in all the required areas to ensure you remain whole and are available to fulfill your mission in life.

When you love your family, you give attention to their needs and desires. Sometimes this means you deprive them of things that may be harmful to them or not in their best interest.

When you love your friends, you are there for them when things are rough and when they are not.

By loving yourself you are able to love others and by doing so, you love God.

44. Show Loyalty.

Some dictionaries refer to loyalty as faithfulness or a devotion to a person, country, group, or cause. When you show loyalty to someone or something, you show that you trust and believe in the individual or cause. You show your support, commitment, dedication, and allegiance. Within the context of showing loyalty, you should ensure the person or cause is deserving and worthy of your loyalty.

Some specific acts of loyalty toward friends and family may include: Not speaking ill of them, especially when they are not around; defending them if someone makes a harsh judgment; treating them the same in all circumstances, regardless of who is around; believing in and encouraging them; and being supportive regardless of circumstances. Some of these same acts apply when showing loyalty to a cause, product, or service.

Showing loyalty to Christ is quite different. You can show your loyalty to Him by not only words of praise, commitment, obedience, and faith, but by actions matching these words. You show Him your loyalty by doing His will, bearing the cross you are given, and living by the fruit of the Spirit as Galatians 5:22-23* tells us. As you go through many of the key behaviors included in this book, you will find they also speak to showing loyalty toward Christ and others.

---

* *"But the fruit of the Spirit is love, joy, peace, forbearance, kindness, goodness, faithfulness, gentleness and self-control. Against such things there is no law."* — *Galatians 5:22-23*

45. Be Memorable.

Farewell to Mattie

I feel as though I'VE lost a kindred spirit from this Earth.
I never met you Mattie but I certainly know your worth.

I watched you on the Oprah show
And read your poetry, too.
Through it I gained a true sense
Of the tender, loving you.

I was moved by your courage
And positive looks at life.
Even though your physical self
Was filled with stress and strife.

Your heartsongs became a comfort
As I read them through and through
They helped me look at life
From a different point of view.

I'll REALLY miss you, Mattie –
A gem, a jewel, a pearl;
I'll think of you quite often
As you look down on our world.

Each time I read your poetry, now,
I'll be reminded of your heart,
And all the songs it gave us
So we're never really apart.

So long, Mattie...

I wrote this in memory of
Mattie J. T. Stepanek
17 July 1990—22 June 2004

We all want to be remembered for the things we do to positively impact the lives of others. You should live your life with a conscious intention of making such a positive difference that those with whom you interact or touch will remember the experience. It doesn't require fame or fortune to be memorable. And don't think that you must die to be memorable. When you take actions to make a positive and enduring difference in the lives of others, it may be difficult for them to forget you — dead or alive!

Hopefully, you will be remembered in a positive sense. If you observe and try to adopt some of the key behaviors discussed in this book, you will be remembered by family, friends, and acquaintances you think matter most and probably by some you never knew you affected. With conscious intention, this can become a real goal to accomplish.

Taking a chance, stepping outside the box, taking initiative, being proactive, setting an example for others to follow, and being courageous all contribute to your being memorable to someone. Even if you do become rich and famous, you will also most likely be memorable, perhaps for how you accomplished that, how you affected others with your fame and fortune, or how you lived such a life. You can choose to live your life to make a difference and be memorable.

"A hundred years from now it will not matter what my bank account was, the sort of house I lived in, or the kind of car I drove... but the world may be different because I was important in the life of a child."   — Forest E. Witcraft

"The LORD has been mindful of us; He will bless us."
— *Psalm 115:12*

46. Be Ever Mindful.

Be ever mindful of how you speak, act, and treat others. Practice conscious intention when you interact with others and the world around you. Be mindful of the outcomes, expected or not, of your thoughts, words, deeds, and actions. Be aware of how others perceive what you do and say, and determine if that is, in fact, your intention.

Be mindful of the needs and desires of your friends, loved ones, and others. This requires being in touch with them on a regular basis and paying attention to what affects them. Determine if there are ways you can help them if they are having adverse experiences that you may have been through or successfully avoided or eliminated.

Be ever mindful of what you put in your body. Monitor your eating habits to ensure you are respecting the body given to you by Christ. Also, give your body the exercise it needs to sustain your requirements for life.

Be ever mindful of your mind and how you nourish it. Pay attention to actions and habits you practice to enhance and improve your mental faculties and capacity. Read a variety of materials and share what you learn with others.

Be ever mindful of your life and how you are living it with regard to your special purpose. Determine why you are here and what other things you can continue to be ever mindful of.

"Do not judge, or you too will be judged. For in the same way you judge others, you will be judged, and with the measure you use, it will be measured to you. Why do you look at the speck of sawdust in someone else's eye and pay no attention to the plank in your own eye? How can you say, 'Let me take the speck out of your eye,' when all the time there is a plank in your own eye? You hypocrite, first take the plank out of your own eye, and then you will see clearly to remove the speck from the other person's eye."
— Matthew 7:1-5

47. Be Non-judging.

Being non-judging means you experience life in an impartial manner, leaving your mind open for all possibilities. A non-judging demeanor allows you to consider all possibilities before coming to an informed conclusion about people, situations, and other experiences.

Being non-judging allows you to be more accepting of others who are different than you. We all have our paradigms that control how we live life and govern our perspectives. Living life with conscious intention allows us to maintain an awareness of this behavior and determine when a paradigm shift may be needed. When you make determinations about others or situations based on appearance, reputation, or hearsay, you deprive yourself of getting both sides. Many times, you are forced to change your opinion of the individual or situation based on information received after your first impression.

Many times we may not even be aware that our behavior constitutes judging. We may see someone dressed differently, wearing too much make-up, speaking strangely, behaving questionably, or just not doing what we expect or the way we would do it. We have no idea what the underlying reasons are for such behavior and we tend to judge others based on their differences rather than embracing them. As the scripture asserts, we must look at ourselves and our own behaviors before we try to judge that of others. When we judge others, we will surely be judged in the same manner.

48. Be Objective.

Generally, the dictionary defines objectivity as:

> "Striving (as far as possible or practicable) to reduce or eliminate biases, prejudices, or subjective evaluations by relying on verifiable data."

When you exercise objectivity, you base your opinions on facts or actual experiences rather than your feelings. You make decisions and derive opinions in an unbiased manner without being influenced by emotions or personal prejudices.

According to Stephen Covey, in his 7 Habits, "We see the world, not as it is, but as we are — or, as we are conditioned to see it." We operate within our paradigms, without knowing when it is beneficial and necessary to shift them to new ones. When we strive to change this, we can become more objective in the way we behave with ourselves and others because we see others as they are and not as we are.

Objectivity is akin to non-judging as we allow ourselves to get the facts and the real story before we decide how to react or respond. When you exercise objectivity, you recognize and accept reality or "what is", without projecting mental models, assumptions, background, or culture, and you respond thoughtfully, deliberately, and effectively.

When you practice objectivity, you develop a reputation for being fair and are respected as such.

49. Be Open-hearted.

Having an open heart allows you to be in touch with your true feelings. You can be honest with yourself as well as others. You are able to give and receive love and to get close to others.

Sometimes we hesitate or refrain from getting close to others for fear of rejection or hurt. We close our hearts to any possibilities of allowing this to happen. As a result, we refrain from living life as it was meant to be. If we fail to reach out to the hearts of others with our own, we will never know what could have become of such an effort.

Having an open heart requires trust in God that He will be right there with you as you endeavor to take actions requiring such faith. As 2 Timothy 1:7 tells us, "For God did not give us a spirit of timidity, but a spirit of power, of love and of self-discipline." God wants us to experience what can come of having an open heart, as He has given us the power and self-discipline to persevere during such times. We must remember that, whatever the outcome, we take away a valuable lesson for continuing to trust that we are not alone as long as our faith in God remains.

Don't think that an open heart will leave you vulnerable to hurt, misuse, or abuse. Having an open heart does not mean you "throw caution to the wind". It means you go into every situation not only with an open heart but also with an open mind to allow you to determine all possibilities. Along with many of the other key behaviors, your eyes will remain open!

50. Be Open-minded.

Very closely related to the previous behavior, an open mind allows us to remain readily acceptable to new suggestions, ideas, influences, or opinions. With an open mind, we are capable of entertaining these new ideas without skepticism or prejudice.

An open mind allows us to be free-thinking while also showing respect for the rights, opinions, and practices of others, even when they are different from our own.

As I discussed in previous books, the thoughts and beliefs you allow to grow in your mind determines how you behave and what you believe. If you have an open mind, you are more willing to consider that anything is possible. You become encouraged that tasks at hand are more doable and you lessen your stress, allowing you to believe things will work out.

Being open-minded allows you to receive information needed to make decisions and live life to its fullest. It also allows you to receive inspiration that can affect the success of your life. It broadens your perspective, thereby allowing you to embrace and experience a range of possibilities not otherwise available with a closed mind.

Being open-minded does not mean you accept everything you hear or experience. Rather, it means you allow your mind to receive, process, or analyze it, and make a determination based on that. A closed mind prevents or limits such possibilities.

51. Have Patience.

All I Need

*God will give me all I need
And show me what to do.
Although I get impatient,
He always gets me through.*

*The courage I need for moving forward
Is there, without a doubt.
Every act He prompts me to take,
I never wonder about.*

*He keeps my best interest at hand
With the highest level of love –
Casting down His wisdom and care,
From His glorious throne above.*

Having patience allows us to tolerate waiting, delays, or frustration without becoming anxious or distressed. Patience lets us control our emotions and impulses and proceed calmly in the face of difficulties, disappointments, or unwanted outcomes.

Exercising patience in a world of instant gratification, supported by today's technology, is difficult, at best, and undesirable at worst. Fortunately, technology has not taken over our entire existence. This leaves other areas where patience is required.

No one can live life and fully enjoy it without some patience. Patience allows us to maintain composure when another car cuts us off in traffic or when someone treats us unfairly. When we pray for things we think we deserve, we must exercise patience—wait on the Lord—while He controls how our lives unfold.

We need patience with our spouses, children, siblings, neighbors, and friends when we have differences that are difficult to resolve.

Having patience prevents us from rushing through important tasks and difficult decisions that affect us and others. We improve our chances of positive outcomes.

For many of us, patience requires faith, practice, focus, and commitment. Without these, while we may get it fast, it may not be what we wanted or even what was needed.

52. Keep A Positive Attitude.

Negative Energy and Positive Thoughts

There's so much negative energy
Existing in our lives today.
Do you find yourself just wishing
You could make it all go away?

But, where could you possibly send it
Without it ending up somewhere
In someone else's peaceful domain
Causing them the same despair?

You pray and pray for some relief
From having to contend
With so much negative energy
Never, ever seeing an end.

You try to have some positive thoughts
To help get through the day.
But someone always comes along
Bringing negative thoughts your way.

You tell yourself you have to choose
a happy, grateful stance
To keep from being affected by
The negativity trance.

You must keep your mind attuned to
Positive, more pleasant things,
To get you through those trying times
And help your heart to sing.

Try a positive tune and a happy dance,
Knowing He holds you near.
Listen to what He tells you.
It's all He wants you to hear.

Keeping a positive attitude means you focus your mind on optimism and opulence, rather than negativity. Your attitude controls the way you view everything around you and that which happens to you. Having a positive attitude will help you to respond to all things in a way which positively benefits you and those around you. A positive attitude puts you in control of yourself. Benefits of a positive attitude include:

- *Better Health* - When optimistic people become ill, they tend to recover more quickly.
- *Less Stress* - How we handle stress depends on our attitude.
- *More Quality Relationships* – You get along better with others.
- *Happier Feelings* – You just plain feel better.
- *More Effectiveness* - Regardless of what type of job you have, the better your attitude, the more you get done.

Applying a positive attitude includes keeping an open mind, practicing self-awareness, and seeking out the good in others rather than dwelling on their negative traits. Positive people believe in themselves, see opportunity everywhere, focus on finding solutions, look for ways to give back, are persistent, and take responsibility for themselves. No one but you can decide what your attitude is. Because you get to make that choice yourself, you have all the power! No matter what someone else does to you or says to you, no one can force you to have an attitude you don't want. Stay Positive!

"I praise the LORD because he does what is right. I sing praises to the LORD Most High." — *Psalm 7:17 NCV*

53. Give Praise.

Giving praise is one of the most powerful forms of positive communication. Opportunities to give praise abound at home, at work, in the community, in church, and in many other interactions we have with others and our Lord and Savior.

Giving praise to God allows us to reflect His glory back to Him. It lets Him know our hearts and the dedication we declare to Him. When we praise God, we give Him credit for the blessings we receive and the forgiveness He shows. Giving praise to God includes thanks to Him for all He does in our lives.

Giving praise to others has the effect of lifting them up and inspiring them to reach higher than they may have thought they could. It lets them know you believe in them and their capability to succeed.

Giving praise can take the form of a compliment on someone's looks or performance. It can mean simply saying Thank You or providing some other token of your appreciation. You can give praise in public or in private. Public praise can involve formal recognition for some significant accomplishment or act. Private praise can include you and the recipient only or, you may want to have a small group with whom to share the praise.

If you are hesitant to give praise or wonder when or if it is appropriate, think about how you felt when you have received it. Everyone wants to receive praise. For that to happen, someone has to give it.

"If you believe, you will receive whatever you ask for in prayer."
— Matthew 21:22

"And this is the confidence which we have before Him, that, if we ask anything according to His will, He hears us. And if we know that He hears us in whatever we ask, we know that we have the requests which we have asked from Him." — 1 John 5:14-15

54. Believe In Prayer.

Believing in prayer creates a life of acceptance for all circumstances and experiences received. When you believe in prayer, and whatever you ask for you do so according to the will of God, you will receive what He has in store for you.

Most think that when you pray, you should get exactly what you ask for. As prayers are answered, we may be confused that what we sometimes get is not exactly what we asked for. This is God's way. He hears our prayers, and answers them in a way that allows us to learn from the experience that is the basis for our prayers. Also, there are times when it may seem like forever between when we asked for something and when it is given to us. Other times we get exactly what we ask for with no gaps in between.

If you doubt that prayer works, try assessing the blessings you have and are receiving, even as you read these words. Prayers are answered when you ask according to God's will, as well as when others ask on your behalf in the same manner.

Believing in prayer includes giving thanks even before your prayers are answered. It also requires you to be aware of the events and experiences in your life that indicate your prayers are being answered. Sometimes, we lose sight of the fact that what we receive is the result of our prayers. As we move closer to God, believing in His blessings for our lives and His answers to our prayers, His voice will become more and more clear as we listen ever so much more.

55. Find Your Purpose.

Our Purpose Here On Earth

If I have touched just one,
My purpose is getting done.
Another two or three or five,
And I'm feeling quite alive!

If those I've touched touch others,
The purpose shall continue.
It doesn't matter the number,
The scope, location, or venue.

The World is ours to change,
Making it a better place to exist –
Not only for us, right here and now,
But for those who will persist.

Our purpose on this Earth
Should be clear – but it's no small feat.
We exist to make some difference here
In the lives of those we meet.

My purpose in life as it has been given me:

To use the influence I have attained and the experiences I have gained, to make a positive and enduring difference, in the lives of as many people with whom I come in contact, by inspiring them to reach their highest potential.   — W. Marie Giles

---

"The purpose of life is a life of purpose."   — Robert Byrne

Discovering the true meaning and purpose of your life can be both liberating and challenging. Liberating because you no longer have to wonder what the purpose of your existence is on this earth, and challenging because you are compelled to find ways to fulfill that purpose.

You were created for a purpose. We all were. It is, therefore, incumbent upon us to find out why we are here, at this time, in this space, and determine how to move toward fulfilling our unique purpose in this life. Finding your purpose gives true meaning to your life. Stephen Covey asks us to imagine attending our own funeral to see how our life will be remembered. How are you writing the story of your life?

Your life is filled with clues that you may or may not have paid much attention to, such as your chosen occupation or career, a particular service you provide to others, specific habits you have developed, skills or talents you have, or comments from others about a certain knack you have, just to name a few.

In order to find your purpose, pay attention to these things and what you do for others—things that bring them joy and give you a feeling of satisfaction. Assess those things in your life that you are passionate about. Delve into self-discovery books and tapes that help reveal to you who you are and why you behave as you do. There are personality tests (Myers-Briggs) and other instruments that can shed light on this key behavior. Finding your purpose will help direct your life and give you the motivation to succeed.

"Respect for ourselves guides our morals; respect for others guides our manners." — *Laurence Sterne*

56. Show Respect.

The importance of showing respect, to yourself and others, is a key part of living your life with conscious intention. When you show others you respect them, you are more likely to gain their respect. When you show respect for yourself, others are more likely to do the same.

There are many ways to show respect and it applies to every interaction we have every day with everyone we meet. When you show respect, you directly acknowledge another's presence and show them they are important to you. Showing respect can involve small gestures and certain body language that reveal your intention. Things like keeping a promise, being on time, listening intently, and not interrupting are just a few. You reflect respect—or the lack thereof—in your behavior, language, tone of voice, and other mannerisms that allow others to "read" you and your intentions.

You show respect to family by valuing their contributions and giving them freedom to express their views and choices. Respect to neighbors include proper care for the appearance of your property and, where possible, avoiding disturbances in the neighborhood. Respect for parents, teachers, and other elders include using "sir" and "ma'am" when communicating with them. You can show respect for yourself by paying attention to your physical and mental health, your emotional requirements, and your spiritual relationships. Respect can help you succeed in life and maintain effective relationships with others.

> *It matters not how strait the gate,*
> *How charged with punishments the scroll.*
> *I am the master of my fate.*
> *I am the captain of my soul.*
>
> — William Ernest Henley
> From: "Invictus"

57. Accept Responsibility.

"I am responsible. Although I may not be able to prevent the worst from happening, I am responsible for my attitude toward the inevitable misfortunes that darken life. Bad things do happen; how I respond to them defines my character and the quality of my life. I can choose to sit in perpetual sadness, immobilized by the gravity of my loss, or I can choose to rise from the pain and treasure the most precious gift I have – life itself." — Walter Anderson

When you accept responsibility for your actions, decisions, outcomes, and impacts, you acknowledge that the choices are yours and not those of others. Accepting responsibility indicates you are willing to enjoy the benefits or accept the consequences of your behavior.

Accepting responsibility for the state of your life, whatever that may be, is essential in acknowledging you are where you are because of past choices you have made in your life. This can empower you to assess these choices and determine how you can make changes to improve or enhance future outcomes. This places you in control of those choices and determines how your future unfolds.

Realizing you can take and accept responsibility may require a leap of faith if you are not accustomed to such behavior. Keep in mind that, while you cannot change or control the behavior or conduct of others, you have control over how you respond to their actions.

Accepting responsibility allows you to dispense with the "blame game" and find better ways of charting and shaping your own life. When you close the door on constantly blaming others for your missteps in life, you open a whole new world of taking control of your words and deeds, revealing how you can direct your life with a clear focus on what you want to accomplish. Go forth and Accept Responsibility!

"Self-discipline begins with the mastery of your thoughts. If you don't control what you think, you can't control what you do. Simply, self-discipline enables you to think first and act afterward."
— Napolean Hill

58. Practice Self-discipline.

Self-discipline refers to control of your impulses, emotions, desires, and behavior. It allows you to focus on gaining more long-term satisfaction and fulfillment from achieving meaningful goals at the expense of some immediate pleasure or instant gratification. It also enables you to make the necessary decisions, take the required actions, and achieve your goals regardless of the obstacles, discomfort, or difficulties that may present along the way.

Self-discipline is a key component in practicing conscious intention to create the life you deserve. It encourages you to overcome any weaknesses, and focus on pursuing your success, despite discouragement from those around you or even your own insecurities.

Self-discipline forces you to set priorities for the things you want most to achieve, acquire, or accomplish in life. As a result, it requires constant reminders, regular practice, and lots of will power to sustain. Sacrifice is also a part of this key behavior. Sometimes you have to forego some desired activity or experience in favor of fulfilling a goal. Self-discipline is evident in successful weight loss, sports, bodybuilding, overcoming addictions, improving personal relationship, and many other areas of life.

As you begin to realize the benefits of self-discipline through your accomplishments, you will continue to improve on the habit to create even more success in your life.

59. Develop Self-awareness.

Seeing Yourself As Others Do

*Seeing yourself differently than others do
Can limit your success.
'Cause others see the good and bad,
Which you might not assess.*

*To see their views, look inside,
Where all your secrets rest.
Be honest with yourself and them.
Put yourself to the test.*

*Seeing yourself as others do
May change your point of view,
Your attitude, your outlook,
The things you say and do.*

*The way you say and hear things
May also change, it's true.
And how you view the world, at large,
May seem to be brand new.*

*Don't hesitate, don't be afraid
To take this chance to know,
How this small step can change your life
And the direction you choose to go.*

*Once you have come to terms
With who you really are,
The rest will fall right into place
And your life will be richer, by far.*

One of the most critical of all the key behaviors discussed in this book is that of self-awareness. It is defined by Encyclopedia Britannica as the "conscious knowledge of one's character, feelings, motives, and desires". From this key behavior, we develop a sense of who we are, why we behave the way we do, and how we can control and monitor our actions and intentions to interact more effectively with others.

Self-awareness puts us in touch with our personality, including strengths, weaknesses, thoughts, beliefs, motivation, and emotions. It allows us to understand others, their perception of us, as well as our attitude and responses to them.

If you consider yourself to be self-aware, yet others see you differently than you see yourself, that may be an indication to embark upon some introspection. Look inside yourself to see what others see in you. You may think it doesn't matter what others think — and in some instances that may be valid. However, if there is a discernible, constant contrast in your views, causing undue conflict or ill-feelings, it may be worth assessing your role in these interactions. Such lack of self-awareness can limit personal growth and success.

Self-awareness helps us to create needed boundaries for ourselves and our relationships with others, thereby reducing adverse interactions and increasing the amount of time we have to create the future we want.

"For I was hungry and you gave me something to eat, I was thirsty and you gave me something to drink, I was a stranger and you invited me in, I needed clothes and you clothed me, I was sick and you looked after me, I was in prison and you came to visit me. Then the righteous will answer him, 'Lord, when did we see you hungry and feed you, or thirsty and give you something to drink? When did we see you a stranger and invite you in, or needing clothes and clothe you? When did we see you sick or in prison and go to visit you?' The King will reply, 'Truly I tell you, whatever you did for one of the least of these brothers and sisters of mine, you did for me.'" — *Matthew 25:35-45*

60. Practice Sharing.

"Share with God's people who are in need. Practice hospitality."
-*Romans 12:13*

Sharing with others indicates a generous and giving spirit. If you have been blessed with gifts and talents, you should be obliged to share the results with others to enrich their lives.

Making charitable donations from our earnings or other possessions is a good way to share with others needing blessings. Tithing is also a form of sharing to enrich our church's mission and support God's teachings.

We all have something we can share in order to benefit someone other than ourselves. We can share knowledge, time, skills, and even a compliment or smile to let others know we care about them and their situations in life.

Sharing reflects and promotes an unselfish demeanor. It encourages us to think about others and not just ourselves. The act of sharing is not made to gain something in return.

Sharing whatever and whenever we can becomes part of our purpose here on Earth. We exist to give of ourselves in a way that promotes the well-being and welfare of others.

Sharing can be done in person or remotely; to one or many; in large or small portions; scheduled or unscheduled; or in any manner that is convenient or appropriate. The most important thing to remember is that we should always be practicing sharing.

61. Show Tenderness.

"Tenderness and kindness are not signs of weakness and despair but manifestations of strength and resolution." -Kahlil Gibran

Acts of tenderness can be as simple as a smile, a hug or embrace, or speaking kind words in a tone that is both comforting and uplifting. Tenderness involves expressing warm and affectionate feelings.

Some of us may have trouble showing tenderness for fear of appearing weak or soft. This is just the opposite. It takes a level of strength to express tenderness to others despite this perceived vulnerability.

Like sharing and other key behaviors discussed in this book, even the smallest act of tenderness can go a long way to promote harmony in relationships. A hand on the shoulder, a pat on the head, or an affectionate whisper in the ear all indicate sincere efforts of showing tenderness. Such acts can serve to endear the deliverer to the recipient.

We all need to experience tenderness on a regular basis. It is essential for us, as humans, to survive and thrive. In marriage, parenting, friendships, and even leadership, showing tenderness is essential for an effective and productive interchange. Tenderness is also essential for the sick, the dying, the rejected, those suffering emotional traumas, the single, the widowed, and divorced and single parents. The burdens that exists in our lives can always be lessened by a little tenderness from someone showing us they care.

"Too often we underestimate the power of a touch, a smile, a kind word, a listening ear, an honest compliment, or the smallest act of caring, all of which have the potential to turn a life around." — Leo F. Buscaglia

If you blurt it out without a pause,
You cannot take it back.
You'll have to live with that outcome
So try to stay on the right track.

62. Think First.

One of the basic premises of conscious intention is to give serious thought to your words and actions before you carry them out. It could make the difference in how you are perceived by others and whether they accept or reject your ideas. Once you move forward with words and actions you usually cannot retract them.

Many times we may act or speak on impulse without first thinking of the outcome. This may be done from anger, hurt, or other emotional feelings. In an effort to live with more conscious intention, these acts can be curtailed. Granted, this requires lots of discipline and practice. You can choose whether it's worth the effort to monitor and control your actions or continue to get the responses you frequently do from impulsive actions.

You may think you don't always have enough time to think about your actions first. Sometimes this may be the case such as in emergencies or threat of life. Believe it or not, you do take time to think first, it may just happen to come a little faster. If you revisit the situation, after its over, you may be surprised to find you acted based on thoughts crossing your mind using the best option available.

Taking the time to think first could spare someone's feelings, improve a relationship, encourage better support, and create a more positive outcome from your interactions than if you had chosen otherwise.

63. Learn To Trust.

This is one of the toughest key behaviors discussed. Trust is fundamental in creating and maintaining meaningful relationships with those you share your life with. Trusting in someone can mean telling them your deepest secrets or simply expecting them to be on time for an appointment. This means there are many degrees and levels of trust.

Learning to trust involves deciding whom to trust, what to include in your trust — or what you are entrusting to others, and at what price you give your trust.

Determining whom to trust involves getting to know a person along with their habits, words, and deeds. You must feel comfortable they will honor your trust in them and they will not betray it.

What or how much you include in your act of trust is up to you. You can entrust some with knowledge in certain areas of your life and others with less or more. Normally, the closer the person is to you and the longer you have known them, the more trust you may give to them. A husband, child, parent, sibling, or close friends may received the highest levels. Others may warrant less.

Determining what it will cost you to trust — or not— can be difficult. Once you decide what you are willing to pay for another's trust, you must be willing to live with the outcome. It could be at the expense of friends, family, or even your livelihood. For this reason, trust should not be given lightly or too quickly.

64. Be Trustworthy.

Being trustworthy allows you to earn and keep another's trust. When you behave with integrity, honesty, and reliability, others are more apt to view you as worthy of their trust.

Other qualities of trustworthiness are fairness, openness, truthfulness, and loyalty. These let others know that you are someone who can be trusted. They are more likely to respect you and want to continue relationships and dealings with you. It also gives you a sense of self-respect.

Being trustworthy requires a commitment from you to honor your promises, carry yourself in a respectful manner, not betray or easily abandon your beliefs, make choices that complement or reflect your value system, and demonstrate a strong moral ethic.

Once you are proven or perceived as being trustworthy, any significant deviation from this behavior could tarnish your reputation, causing you to have to re-earn trust. In this case, get yourself back on track by admitting to your mistake and continuing your commitment as before. While you may not be able to regain the trust of all, many will see your efforts as sincere and may be willing to give you another chance.

"Trust is the highest form of human motivation. It brings out the very best in people." — *Stephen Covey*

65. Try Harder.

Sometimes we may have the tendency to give up on something because it seems too difficult, takes too long, moves too slowly, or we just don't see the results we want. This is the time to try harder and determine to go a little further to get a glimpse of the light at the end of the tunnel.

If you commit yourself to seeing something through, to accomplish goals you set for yourself, this gives you the strength and fortitude to try harder. This does not mean pushing yourself beyond what you know to be your true limit.

Trying harder means reaching within yourself to determine if you have a little more you can give or a little further you can go. It means knowing the satisfaction you will receive in pushing yourself a little harder than you normally do, but without going so far it will destroy you.

Trying harder requires a knowledge of self — a conscious awareness of who you are and what you are capable of. It means following God's intention for your life and being in touch with Him by accepting how far He wants you to go and how hard He wants you to try.

Trying harder does not refer to a comparison between you and someone else. It reflects giving YOUR personal best to achieve the very best you can.

66. Have Some Understanding.

Stephen Covey's fifth habit, "Seek first to understand, then to be understood" is what comes to mind with this key behavior. We all want others to understand us. We think we deserve it. We want to be who we are and let the others know and accept it. However, we can best achieve this by putting forth the effort to listen and understand others as we want to be understood ourselves.

You never know what someone else is experiencing when they react to you or treat you in a manner you consider unacceptable. Perhaps they have just suffered the loss of a loved-one, a job, or a major opportunity. They may just need someone to not just react to their behavior but, rather, see what could be internal to their outward actions or words.

Having some understanding does not mean you accept or condone the behavior. It means you can see it to be different and not personal toward you. You relate to the words or actions of others from their point of reference, not your own. This may require better listening to others and less to yourself during the interaction. When you listen to yourself, you tend to form responses based on your prejudice or paradigm rather than objectivity.

Having understanding may not always prevent or resolve conflicts, but it can help reach a mutually acceptable compromise.

"In an argument, the test of wisdom is the ability to summarize the other person's view before starting one's own." — *Haim Ginott*

67. Value Life.

Valuing your life allows you to live it to its fullest. You pay attention to what matters most to you as well as how to enhance the life of others. How you live your life could be an indication of just how much you value it.

Balancing the key dimensions of your life (physical, mental, emotional, and spiritual) is one way to show that you value it. Encouraging others to do the same lets them know you value their life as well.

Live your life in such a way that shows you respect and appreciate being alive. Treat others in your life with dignity and respect to let them know you value and appreciate them.

Finding and fulfilling your true purpose in life is another way to reflect how much you value your existence. Sharing your gifts and talents with others who can benefit from them is part of this process.

Taking time to review the key behaviors in this book indicates your interest in living with conscious intention. This also shows the value you hold on your life and how you can contribute to the value of the lives of others.

"If my life is of no value to my friends, then it is of no value to me." — Joseph Smith

"A man who dares to waste one hour of life has not discovered the value of life." — Charles Darwin

68. Show Willingness.

Showing willingness indicates your positive attitude to move forward and accomplish the things you wish to in life. You give up being reluctant to act in situations that are in your best interest as well that of others.

Showing willingness means we are enthusiastic, eager, and cheerful about what we undertake that can improve our lives and those of others. Any change in life requires willingness. You must also be ready to continually maintain commitment to the new way resulting from the change, for as long as you want that change to remain.

When you show willingness in your life pursuits, you improve your chances of success. A willing attitude is more apt to get you what you seek in life far more than unwillingness.

As you progress through life, keep in mind areas where showing willingness can benefit you and others. Be open to the ideas of others and don't hesitate to share what you know. Show your willingness to learn from others and apply that knowledge or experience.

Showing willingness is one more key behavior that can improve your conscious intention, making the world a better place for us all.

"Now finish the work, so that your eager willingness to do it may be matched by your completion of it, according to your means."
— 2 Corinthians 8:11

69. Gain Wisdom.

Gaining wisdom is different from gaining knowledge. To know something does not make you wise. When you gain wisdom you are able to use the knowledge you have in ways that are most beneficial to you and others.

With wisdom, you have a deep understanding and realization of people, things, events, or situations, which results in your ability to apply perceptions, judgments, and actions based on this understanding. It often requires control of your emotional reactions so that general principles, reason, and knowledge prevail.

Gaining wisdom can provide an open-minded, more serene, and level-headed approach to living. It leads us to seek self-growth and personal development, as well as build better relationships and expand our spiritual nature. It makes life more meaningful.

Only you can gain wisdom for yourself. No one can make you wise or make you not wise. It's up to you. When you see, hear, or experience a valuable lesson, it's up to you to learn from it. Put what you have learned into practice or you will never be wise.

"Knowledge is a process of piling up facts; wisdom lies in their simplification."   — *Martin Fischer*

"Do not forsake wisdom, and she will protect you; love her, and she will watch over you. Wisdom is supreme; therefore get wisdom. Though it cost all you have, get understanding."
               — *Proverbs 4:6-7*

70. Maintain A Sense Of Wonder.

Double Digit

I'm 10, I'm 10!
No longer in
The single-digit age.

I'm 10, I'm 10
I've reach the top
The world is now my stage!

Our sense of wonder reflects our feelings of joy, excitement, and mystery of the world we live in. It is defined by things like emotion aroused by something awe-inspiring, astounding, or marvelous; the quality of amazed admiration; attention or astonishment at something awesomely mysterious or new to one's experience; or a state in which you want to learn more about something.

Our sense of wonder allows us to experience the world with admiration, curiosity, surprise, and awe. It separates us from the drudgery or monotony of repetitive actions and technology-controlled behavior that forces us to abandon the beauty and meaning of nature and all it has to offer.

By focusing more on what's happening around us, and less on the televisions, computers, and other technology, we get to enjoy those special moments, events, and people in our lives that we would otherwise miss. Things like the beauty and wonder of nature, time spent with a child—marveling at how they see the world, noticing the little things someone does or how they relate, becoming a lifelong student, and exploring the world — even if you have to do so vicariously, can all help maintain our sense of wonder. Try your hand at creativity, such as writing, painting, dancing, or learning a craft. You may amaze yourself.

Cultivate and maintain a sense of wonder. It will improve your quality of life.

"He who can no longer pause to wonder and stand rapt in awe, is as good as dead; his eyes are closed." — *Albert Einstein*

71. Work Harder.

Whatever you choose to endeavor, the outcome will be more rewarding if you work harder. Most of us feel we already work hard for the things we want out of life. This key behavior challenges you to go further, especially if you seem to be getting less or you're not satisfied with where you've settled.

Working harder requires you to assess just how hard you are currently working and whether the outcome satisfies you. If it does, you may already be working as hard as you need to. On the other hand, if you desire more out of your job, education, fitness, health, craft, parenting, hobby, or any other activity, working harder could get you there.

Working harder is not just about physical strength. It's also about brains and intelligence. You must have a clear picture of what you are pursuing, the methods, tools, and techniques to be used, and the time required to make it happen.

While working harder may have different meanings for different people, it remains that only you can determine how much harder you have to work in order to improve your past outcomes. Key and meaningful achievements of your goals require you to fall in love with hard work. Working harder makes the difference.

"I'm a great believer in luck and I find the harder I work, the more I have of it." — *Thomas Jefferson*

"There is no substitute for hard work." — *Thomas Alva Edison*

"As long as you feel young at heart, age is just a number."
— Alokoa Yeseng

72. Stay Young At Heart.

"And if you should survive to 105
Look at all you'll derive out of being alive
Then here is the best part, you have a head start
If you are among the very young at heart."

— Frank Sinatra (from the song "Young At Heart")

Regardless of how old you get, you can always stay young at heart. It comes down to how you perceive yourself, your habits, thoughts, and practices. Your biological or chronological age need not determine how young you feel.

Finding ways to stay young at heart is not as hard as you may think. Try staying active, spending time with children, looking for things to make you smile and laugh often, and refraining from grumbling or complaining. Never be ashamed of your age. Instead, celebrate it. Find your passion and engage in it. Maintain a positive attitude and never stop learning. Pay attention to your eating and exercise habits, making them work for and not against you.

Believing that you are as young as you feel encourages you to act younger, feel younger, and even look younger. Your attitude will remain modern as you stay abreast of current trends, adapt to changes in technology, and stay in touch with the "younger" generation. Your thoughts can keep you young by being open-minded. We sometimes show our true age when we get fixed in our opinions and perspectives.

Take a look around at those older than you who appear younger than they are. See how they maintain the state of staying young at heart and try to emulate them.

Take steps now to maximize your life and determine what you can do to stay young at heart.

73. Learn To Yield.

Learning to yield does not mean you give in or give up. It means you know when to let something go and move on. It also means being considerate of others—whether allowing them to speak first in conversations, have the right-of-way in traffic, or go first in line at the grocery. The message here is don't feel you always have to be first.

Learning to yield also refers to letting God take care of our problems and refraining from interfering with His methods and lessons. We all tend to think we can do it ourselves. We want to control our lives and the situations presented to us. Learning to yield to our Savior shows that we trust His will in every situation of our lives.

Learning to yield in relationships is key to attaining harmony and a more peaceful existence. With spouses, children, neighbors, co-workers, and others, we don't always have to prove we are right. Some situations are not worth the sacrifice of good relations. We may end up being right but with the unintended result of being unhappy. Which is more important to you?

Sometimes we find that when we yield to the needs and desires of others, we may end up reaping more benefits than we imagined.

"Now then," said Joshua, "throw away the foreign gods that are among you and yield your hearts to the LORD, the God of Israel."
— Joshua 24:23

"Never be lacking in zeal, but keep your spiritual fervor, serving the Lord." — Romans 12:11

74. Maintain Zeal.

The dictionary defines zeal as "passionate devotion to or interest in a cause or subject". Different versions of the Bible refer to it as earnest, eager, or committed. In either case, it represents a level of excitement and enthusiasm about how you approach life, that can move you forward toward accomplishing your goals.

Maintaining zeal in your relationships with family and friends can make life more meaningful and full of joy. Embracing every facet of your life with zeal helps you maintain a positive attitude and a feeling that anything is possible.

Being zealous for God is what Scripture directs. When we bring such enthusiasm to the manner in which we view and serve Him, we are assured of a well-lived existence. Our zeal for Him ensures we give Him all the glory, making Him the center of our very existence. It lets us trust that we can do all things through Christ who strengthens us.

Maintaining zeal is a very important key behavior that benefits the world in which we live. Our zeal for living a purposeful life, trusting in Christ, relating to family and friends, and focusing on positive outcomes can only contribute to the betterment of all. Imagine if this could be multiplied all over the world. The results would be true enrichment of our own lives as well as that of this wonderful world we live in.

"It is fine to be zealous, provided the purpose is good, and to be so always, not just when I am with you." — *Galatians 4:18*

After Word

I truly hope you have enjoyed and benefited from reading this book. It was my conscious intention to give you lots to think about as you continue to go through life, interacting with many different people and situations. None of us are expected to be consciously intentional every minute of every day. However, some small, deliberate changes in our behavior, reflecting what we know, can certainly benefit not only ourselves but also the world we value and choose to live in.

As you allow this message to soak in, refer back to those behaviors that most interest or intrigue you. Take time to get to know how they apply to you and how they can improve your relationships with God, family, friends, co-workers, community members, and the church.

Thanks for taking the time to discover what I have to say.

W. Marie Giles
mgileswb@att.net

Additional Resources

The following books have contributed to my journey and may prove useful to you in your journey of self-discovery.

Eckhart Tolle
- A New Earth: Awakening To Your Life's Purpose,
- The Power of Now

Mark Nepo
- The Book of Awakening

Stephen R. Covey
- The Seven Habits of Highly Effective People
- First Things First (with A. Roger Merrill and Rebecca R. Merrill)
- Living the 7 Habits
- Principle-Centered Leadership
- The 8th Habit

Don Miguel Ruiz
- The Four Agreements
- The Four Agreements Companion Book
- The Mastery of Love
- The Fifth Agreement

Colin Creel
- Navigating Your Calling and Career

William P. Young
- The Shack

Andy Andrews
- The Noticer
- The Butterfly Effect

Carol Adrienne
- The Purpose of Your Life

Les Brown
- Live Your Dreams

T.D. Jakes
- Maximize the Moment

Denis Waitley
- The Psychology of Winning

Brian Tracy
- The Psychology of Achievement

Alan Kraft
- Good News For Those Trying Harder

Gary Zukav
- The Seat of the Soul
- Soul Stories
- The Heart of the Soul

Dr. Viktor E. Frankl
- Man's Search for Meaning

John C. Maxwell
- Make Today Count
- Today Matters
- The Maxwell Daily Reader

Vernice Amour
- Zero to Breakthrough

Peter Bregman
- 18 Minutes

Cheryl Richardson
- Take Time for Your Life
- Life Makeovers

Florence Littauer
- It Takes So Little to Be Above Average
- Your Personality Tree

Dr. John M. Oldham and Lois B. Morris
- The New Personality Self-Portrait—Why You Think, Work, Love, and Act the Way You Do

Malcolm Gladwell
- Blink
- The Tipping Point

Dr. Phil McGraw
- Life Strategies
- Getting Real
- Self Matters

David Allen
- Getting Things Done

Joel Osteen
- Your Best Life Now
- Become A Better You
- It's Your Time: Activate Your Faith, Achieve Your Dreams, and Increase in God's Favor
- Every Day A Friday

David Hutchens and Barry Rellaford
- A Slice of Trust

Guideposts (Annual)
- Daily Guideposts: A spirit-lifting /devotional

Philip Yancy and Brenda Quinn
- Meet the Bible: A panorama of God's word in 366 daily readings and reflections

Gay Hendricks
- Five Wishes: How answering one question can make your dreams come true

Brenda Pace and Carol McGlothlin
- The One Year Yellow Ribbon Devotional

Rhonda Byrne
- The Secret

Jack Canfield
- Key to Living the Law of Attraction

Barack Obama
- The Audacity of Hope
- Dreams From My Father

Mary E. Allen
- 12 Weeks to Living A Life YOU Love

www.ingramcontent.com/pod-product-compliance
Lightning Source LLC
LaVergne TN
LVHW051556070426
835507LV00021B/2615